A Gift FOR
you —
With our
Compliments

Eden Grove
Press

THEY WILL ENDURE

FORTY PORTRAITS ARE ASSEMBLED HERE IN CONCISE, DEEPLY
PONDERED RECOLLECTIONS WHICH CONFIRM MOVINGLY HOW MEMORY
AND EMOTION CAN PRODUCE A DIMENSION ONLY A PARTICULAR
SON OR DAUGHTER COULD RENDER. VARIETY AND SINGULARITY GIVE
THIS SLENDER VOLUME THE CAPACITY TO SURPRISE AND ENTHRALL.
THE READER WILL DISCOVER IN WORDS AND PHOTOGRAPHS HOW
UNEXPECTEDLY AVAILABLE THE PAST MAY BE, AND HOW ELUSIVE –
OFTEN TELLING US AS MUCH ABOUT THE WRITER AS THE ABSENT
FATHER. EXAMINED TOGETHER THOSE BRIEF ENCOUNTERS DO NOT
EASILY DRIFT AWAY. THEY WILL ENDURE.

STANLEY E. FLINK IS THE AUTHOR OF SEVERAL BOOKS, INCLUDING *SENITINEL UNDER SIEGE, THE TRIUMPHS AND TROUBLES OF AMERICAN PRESS*. HE IS A FORMER CORRESPONDENT FOR *LIFE MAGAZINE NEWS PRODUCER* FOR NBC AND CBS; SENIOR ADVISOR TO YALE UNIVERSITY AND NEW YORK UNIVERSITY CENTER'S FOR MEDIA AND JOURNALISM, INCLUDING FIRST LECTURER FOR THE *LIFELONG LEARNING DISTINGUISHED LECTURE SERIES*.

FORTY SONS AND DAUGHTERS
FINDING FATHER WITHIN

ELM GROVE

Forty Sons and Daughters
Finding Father Within

Direct any inquiries to:

Elm Grove Press, LLC
PO Box 153
Old Mystic, CT 06372
elmgrovepress.org

ISBN: 978-1-9408-6303-0

Printed in the USA

FORTY SONS AND DAUGHTERS FINDING FATHER WITHIN

JESS MAGHAN & SAM LINDBERG

Preface

Leaning over the coffin, saying my final good-bye, I reached in and adjusted my father's necktie, studying his face for one last time. Who was this man that I will never see again and have known my entire life? As we ponder our life and lineage, this question returns many times, whether you hold your father as your anchor and standard-bearer in life, as your coach and friend, or as an enigmatic man who was mostly absent. Or perhaps it is a mix of all these aspects. The grace of time has buffered my days with my father. I now realize that he will remain a constant factor in my life, helping me to understand that it is indeed not the answers we seek in life but the questions we ask that are important. Those questions surrounding my father are now guiding my work and the quality of my interactions with others, inculcating, as it does for everyone else, an acute awareness of who we are and why we do what we do. The yearning we all have to connect with our father is the premise and catalyst of this book.

Each participant brought a spark to the darkness. Not one of them came empty-handed. A few found the light too bright and wanted it dimmed or turned off completely, but the commitment for all of them was absolute. It is clear to me now that a father and each of his children remain on separate paths. For instance, most of us ended up unconsciously emulating our fathers, while working very hard at rejecting them in the youthful arrogance of doing things our own way. Throughout this book the gift of letting go and just accepting life in the raw has surfaced as a magic formula and, in one way or another, these narratives carry a curiously contagious and redeeming spirit.

In reading these entries, you may find yourself circling the wagons, taking a needed rest, and pausing to gaze at the stars. And perhaps for the first time, you may listen to what was not being said in what was being said – what was hidden and why. Along with joyous memories of family, home and humor in the comfort of the front porch swing come memories of separations, deaths and the lessons from living with loss. And intriguingly, there is awareness that the forces sifting our memories are so powerful that they, themselves, are often as fascinating as the memory itself. I trust the immediacy of these forty father portrayals will enable you, the reader, to tap into the familiar yearning all sons and daughters have to connect with the man who started them on their life's journey and is irrevocably anchored at the very center of their being. The man we call father.

Jess Maghan
Chester, Connecticut
20 April, 2015

Appreciation

To The Reader:

The power of this book is derived from the inspiring force and patience of the forty sons and daughters who brought forth reflections of their fathers and themselves. Their writings have sprouted wings under the energized focus of writer-author, CEO Ruth Crocker of Elm Grove Press.

Her team, including designer Mark Starr, have mounted a format of our Boolean algebra theorem of 'two false equal one truth' which became the staging steps for these sons and daughters in composing their 'Father' paragraphs. And significantly, Sam Lindberg's sensitive photography, embracing the enlightening spirit nestled in each entry.

As for me, this book has long stood in the corner of my heart, silently waiting to deliver unsaid messages between my own father and myself. Messages that have now been discovered through the humanity of these collective voices, willing to tell the truth and see what happens, in recording their journey of finding father in their inner self.

As for me, it was to be my 'reach' in truly knowing my father. I think he would have been pleased that it was written. It is full of the unsaid that hangs in a room, hangs in a house, and hangs in a person. Today, I own the yearning to know the whole story as a gift of no longer being incomplete. I have insights now that I can go to and come from.

Remember always! Your father had a father, and his father had one too! So how unique are we? Acceptance is the key, and take note, we used a curved mirror in constantly coinciding with the premise of this book throughout.

Jess Maghan

The Essays and Their Authors

Blue Collar Guy

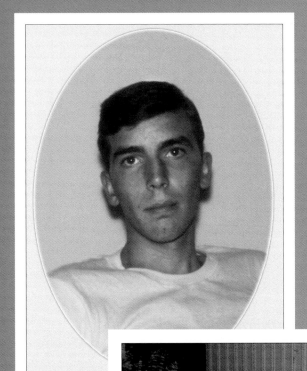

For me, harnessing the good qualities Dad passed down is not a difficult task. My Dad was a "blue collar guy" with a white collar job. He took pride in what he had achieved and what he had overcome in life. He loved our home and enjoyed working around the house. As a seventeen-year-old high school dropout, he joined the army, spent four years in Vietnam and became an officer. After his discharge he enrolled in college, majoring in accounting and graduating magna cum laude. He then became a successful CPA. Although he was a genuine and good-natured person, in many ways he was a stranger to himself and others. He had a lot of personal demons and was always torn between his demons and his family. As a result of his heavy drinking, he could easily become outspoken and unreasonably stubborn. One day when I got home from school, there was a police officer waiting to report that Dad had been hit by a car. Even though extremely ill, he had tried to walk to buy cigarettes. According to the police, he was thrown twenty-five feet in the air and both his legs were broken. Later Dad had to stay in an assisted living facility because his mental state was declining. We would visit him and often he didn't remember who we were. When Dad finally told me he was dying, I was crushed. I had always looked at him as Superman, indestructible. When he died, I didn't believe it at first and was angry for many years. I still miss him every day. My Dad grew up defending his mother and brother from his abusive father. I realize now that it was in 1993, after Dad was gone and I was thirteen, that like him I began taking care of my mother and brother with much the same feeling of responsibility for protecting them. What else could I do?

My Father

S omehow I feel that I have the double-strength of a father in me and when the time comes for me to be a real one, it will be easy. At my brother's junior prom the parents were photographing their kids and it was me (as a surrogate father) being photographed with my brother and his date. Maybe I can attribute my surrogate dad role to always feeling older than I was. This had spilled over into other aspects of my life as well. Any time I'd see myself as being favored in any way, I'd always try to move the spotlight away from myself and shift the focus onto people who needed reinforcement. I also never get caught up in what people think about me and this has made me happier in general. I have completed my university degree in accounting and I am now in the final process for CPA certification. More importantly I also realize my "surrogate father" role throughout my teenage years was also a heavy emotional burden. I had become too careful at staying responsible and taking care of others. The good and bad things that made up my father's short life, the futility of unspoken fear and his stubbornness in refusing to confront his demons are now but indelible memories. Gratefully I learned early in life that even the toughest men need help and, most importantly, it takes the strength of humility to escape from false pride. These are lessons I will never forget.

Adam Barth

Myself

Sandhog

My Father

Beginning in the early 1920s, in a hostile, segregated, rural town in Georgia, an eight-year-old colored boy, my father, worked and raised himself. He never went to school. He never had a book or toy. He never had a loving family. He never had someone to hug and kiss him. In fact, he never had anything that most of us take for granted. I always looked up to my father for his awesome physical strength and his uncanny ability to fix anything from a broken automobile to my bicycle chain, or even in later years, my shotgun. I remember the Christmas morning when I was eight years old, waking up to find my only gift to be an odd-looking sailor suit instead of the toys I had longed for. Since I was an only child, my list had been quite long. I overheard my normally quiet mother loudly scolding my father for gambling away his paycheck and bringing home that pitiful gift for me. I added insult to injury when I stated that this was the worst Christmas I ever had. I do not remember my father's reaction. Twenty years earlier, he had "celebrated" his eighth Christmas as a homeless and abandoned child whose own father had just been killed a few weeks earlier. His mother had died two years earlier in childbirth. His uncles and aunts took in each of his four siblings and raised them. For some unknown reason, my father was left to roam the streets. To survive, for him, meant living under houses at night to keep warm and working odd jobs during the day in order to eat. No one wanted him. In 1935, he managed to migrate to New York and found work as a "Sandhog" in the vast, cold and damp tunnels of the great Aqueduct at Croton, New York. Now, these sixty years later, I hold fast to the haunting memory of that pitiful sailor suit on Christmas day so many years ago.

Addis Taylor

My father was truly "a self-made man," the proverbial phoenix bird, recreating himself from the ashes of burnout in being a black man deep in Jim Crow's South. As a child I learned early on of the blunt futility of trying to bring my problems to my father. His solution to every problem I had was very simple: "Kids have no problems." My father felt that all I had to do in life was to go to school and get good grades. I compensated by keeping my problems to myself just as he had done; I worked them out for myself. Today my adult son and I are often estranged because he feels that I have always been indifferent to his problems. On the surface I am an outgoing person, but instinctively I keep everything to myself. When my children would come to me with a problem, I too replied with Dad's mantra: "A kid's problem is not a real problem." The irony in all of this is that I am a trained dispute resolution professional. I have been well paid to assist organizations by teaching their personnel how to resolve disputes, and I have assisted many by resolving their problems. But, actually, I am the shoemaker whose family had no shoes, because he had no time to listen to them. Upon completion of my Ph.D., I proudly handed a copy of my dissertation to my father and was stunned by his pain in noting that I had omitted "Jr." – our father-son generational link – from my name on the title page. There, in the glow of that hard-earned recognition, we stood in the naked silence of misunderstanding, two men permanently wounded by years of undelivered communication.

Myself

Blue

When my older sister was eighteen months old my mother, with great sadness, left her in England and went to join my father in Nigeria where he worked in the education department. It was expected of her to join him in his foreign service, but climate in West Africa was too dangerous for children. Mother was twenty-five when they married. She considered herself to be "on the shelf" since no one else had asked her, and since Tom kept asking her, she decided to finally say yes! Tom was an academic man, small with light hair and green eyes, and a great wit which was usually used at other people's expense. He wrote excellent letters and Mother always said she liked him best on paper. I don't remember meeting him until I was about five. He was on leave and came into our bedroom and capered about singing and doing odd dances. I thought, "Who is this, and why is he here?" I never felt close to him and I don't think he liked me much. In Nigeria Mother met a man whom I really loved. I wished he was my father and I called him "Blue." He and Mother rode horses together and talked animatedly, and had so much mutual admiration. When Mother came back to England, she met Blue's mother and they decided to buy a large house together. So when Blue was home on leave he came to our house. I remember running into his bedroom as soon as I woke, clambering onto his bed and sitting on his chest. He taught me to ride and climb trees. Tall, dark and handsome, he carried me on his shoulders and held me in his arms when he danced the tango to the wind-up gramophone in the nursery.

My Father

When Mother died, I had a letter from Blue's daughter saying that she had been told by two different people that Blue was my father. Though the news came as a shock, it fulfilled what I'd always hoped was true. So what is my legacy from my two fathers? With my father, Tom, I share a love of books and feeling of words. Now I understand his character better and why he never played with us, finding it easier to communicate with children as if they were adults. He was always telling me that I was too noisy and talkative. Throughout my life, he and my mother slept at opposite ends of the house. My other father, Blue, will always waken in me a feeling of love and closeness. When I was grown up, I never lived with him so I never lost the feelings of romance he wakened in me. I last saw him in the hospital when he had cancer. I knew he would look different so I told myself to look at his hands, which were long and brown and beautiful. When I got to his bed, a hand reached round the curtain and held me. We talked and talked. When I left he said, "Please bring your lovely mother to see me." I promised I would, but couldn't. I took her to his funeral instead.

Ruth Hill

Myself

Only Me

My father has been dead so long that I have nothing of him but fragments. Most of my childhood recollections of me and him were about us going somewhere together. Dad drove a great deal in his work supervising the ceiling installation crews. During WWII, he had the largest gas-ration allotted to a non-clergy civilian. Despite that, Father especially liked to drive on our vacations to northern Michigan or Canada north of Lake Superior. One of the most reassuring sounds of my childhood came when I was stretched out sleeping in the back seat of the car as he drove at night. Whenever I awoke, I heard the "click, click, click" from the button on the floor as he switched the lights back and forth from bright to dim. Although often uncommunicative, I could gauge a little of his feelings toward me by the presents I received: a football helmet, Lincoln Logs, a chemistry set. The Christmas I was nine, he gave me a Lionel diesel locomotive train with freight cars, an oil tanker, and a caboose, but best of all, a milk car. When you pushed a button, a man shoved milk cans out onto the station platform. Father also built a plywood table in my bedroom, stained it green and affixed the tracks, complete with bridges, stations and switches. Dad worked a lot, even at home where he kept everything he needed in the garage. Sometimes I sat near him when he worked there and we talked, and I would help with tasks I was big enough to do. We also did things together during his free time, but often he was so tired that he fell asleep while listening to the radio. He loved children and was always willing to baby-sit for our friends with young children. I remember especially how he loved, deeply, his own brothers and sisters. Being the youngest of ten, I believe he expected a family very much like his own. But, if he wanted a big family, he didn't get it. There was only me.

My Father

I look down at my hands and arms, and I see my father's. When my father talked with me, it was always of practical matters and to this day it is in practical matters that I feel him most with me. I tell my daughter how to mow grass properly and paint flawlessly. When I start to make some repair or work in the garden, I find myself down in the dirt spending too much time getting some small detail absolutely correct and even come back months later if it doesn't please me. If I had my idea of a perfect world, I would ask one more favor of my father. I want him to have a grave. He had his ashes scattered on a lake in Florida. I'd like a place we could be alone together just as in the past. He could get to know his granddaughter. In describing her to my father, I might discover something that had escaped me all my life. As a child, you develop a picture of your father. Then, when you get older, you learn something that destroys that picture. After my parents retired and moved to Florida, they became good friends with a local couple that had a pool table. When I visited, we all played pool and would always lose to Dad. Eventually, my father told us that as a teenager, he used to go into town and play pool. He learned to play so well that he made money betting on the games. That was not the father I knew. If Dad could come back some morning, what would I say? What would I ask? If he came so early that the door was locked, and he knocked, what would I say?

Barry C. Fox

Myself

I realized almost from birth that my siblings and I were brought into the world as a cure for the near annihilation of the generation before us. We took for granted talk of death at the dinner table, only played with children of other refugees, and routinely heard many languages among our parents' friends. These survivors of Hitler's concentration camps could not hide their damage; to us it was just a normal aspect of parenthood. My father rarely talked about his experiences, but openly wore the scars. He used to tell me, "Mankind is a cruel hoax God played upon this earth." My father was a tailor and designer/pattern maker for a women's coat-and-suit company. He would walk my sister and me through clothing stores to examine the current season's line, look at buttonholes, zippers and seams. Sometimes he would shake his head in disgust and say, "This is not a seam, it's a crime!" Of his three children I somehow reached the deepest part of him, maybe through my music or constant questions about his homeland. Most likely it was his inability to equally love more than one person at a time. I got as much out of him as he could spare. He confided in me often, although I was inappropriate for the therapist role he assigned me. He told me when I was fifteen that he would never allow himself to be put in a nursing home. His definition of growing old was "some bastard who doesn't care about you, making decisions about your body and mind. That is the kind of growing old I refuse to do again," he declared, already having had enough with the Nazis. His first attempt at suicide failed; he took an overdose of Xanax after a Passover Seder meal. He said he planned it that way so no one would have to pay extra to travel to his funeral. When he shot himself in the head in 2000, I was not surprised. What did surprise me was that even though I had known for a long time that he would most likely take his own life – his ultimate act of control – my grief was no less painful.

My Father

Cruel Hoax

As long as I can remember, I assumed the role of comedian in my family. It was obvious, though maybe never stated in words, that we (my siblings and I) were the antidote to Hitler's destruction. So if you look at early pictures of my brother, sister and me, you will understand why we named ourselves the worried smilers. We were cheerful when our parents couldn't be, almost as a prescription to their darkness. My mother, a master of "denial and moving on" (which was her survival concealed in a pasted-on postwar smile), and my father always looked resigned in family photos. Only at his designer's table or his sewing machine did he seem at home. I never realized that this approach to work, to his creations, would leak out of his tight-lipped being into me. Only since his suicide have I realized the impact of my family history. I named my musical group Veretski Pass, after the mountain pass in the Carpathians where my dad was born. I spend my time researching and playing music from that region, reforming it, mixing it with styles of surrounding cultures, playing it with a Jewish accent. I have made it my goal to put new, reformed, but traditional music back into the Jewish repertoire. I have taken his habit of hovering over a work, cutting, sewing parts until I am satisfied enough with a tune that I could almost wear it. But when someone asks me about the pain and sadness that is mixed into each stroke of my bow, I become like him, smiling tight lipped, and claim, "It's just music." The lineage that connects me with the loss that my parents suffered and later with the violent loss of my father is like a rough woolen coat that is too heavy to wear. Music is my way of wearing a few threads, which I cling to desperately and privately

Cookie Segelstein

Myself

11

M alcolm Frederick Calder was born in 1907 in the tiny New Zealand farm town of Temuka, where his father ran a bicycle repair shop and where a local farmer built, flew and crashed a flimsy airplane years before the Wright Brothers. Caught in the global chaos of the Great Depression and the distilling menace of WWII, Malcolm (surely inspired by that first flight in Temuka) volunteered for the Royal Air Force in England and was assigned to the huge deployment for the coming Battle of Britain in 1940. His outstanding military and leadership prowess catapulted him back to help build the Royal New Zealand Air Force. He was destined to become Chairman of the Joint Chiefs of Staff of the armed forces of New Zealand. I desperately wanted to follow my father into the Air Force, but poor eyesight derailed this dream. His response to the depths of my disappointment was to immediately steer me into a professional career in aeronautical engineering. Father's mind was insatiable in its dexterity for self-nurturing through literature, painting, music, rugby and walking in the countryside. He loved fly-fishing and we spent many hours in the mighty Tongariro River, where he patiently gifted me with his honed expertise in how to "tie a fly and finesse a cast." His impeccable, yet gentle, probity reigned over our lives, instilling in us to always be "family" in the midst of military separation, distance and danger. On what was to become our final parting, the last day of a glorious summer holiday in 1976, he surprised us by dressing immaculately, complete with squadron tie. As we drove away, he stood straight as an arrow, smiled and slowly saluted. Later, when complications arose from a surgery, he insisted he would soon be on the mend, but, clearly, he'd foreseen the end and wanted us to remember that final salute. At his funeral, his Chief of Air Staff successor saluted him as "The Queen's Gentle Soldier," a hero of over 35 years in Her Majesty's Service in two air forces of the Commonwealth.

Aviator Mind

My Father

Richard Calder

If there ever was a man comfortable with himself, it was my father. His aviator mind, always on target, signaled his motto in life: "There is no such thing as failure. There is only feedback!" He could soar above any problem and spot a solution from the heights of pure understanding. I can now clearly see that his motto continues to champion my family and career. His spirit prevails in our clan, fostering a strong connectedness between (and with) our four children, now chasing the world in challenge and creativity. Early in life, my sister and I were given to understand that we were young adults operating out of a tribal bond thriving on the connectedness enjoyed by each generation. I have discovered that, with this linkage, our home will never be an empty nest. It has all come together, as if by magic, here in Connecticut, where we now have our own pocket of the New Zealand countryside, complete with chicken pens and a small flock of sheep sequestered under the shade of giant maple and fir trees. And most of all, now and again, up there in the clouds, I can spot father saluting his adventurous and cohesive family, who are always-at-home, whether together or alone.

Myself

After Vietnam my dad came home to my mom and a new son, my brother, and I followed eighteen months later. I really didn't get to know my dad until after my parents divorced, when I was twelve years old and would spend weekends with him. Those days were the most fulfilling of my young life and I am still wrapped in the magic of them. I remember his strong paw-like hands when he was consoling me on the loss of our dog, Budweiser. Dad could grab your inner soul and shelter it. Years later, when I returned from serving in Desert Storm, Dad was the first person I called and I remember how he greeted me with his bright eyes, a hug, a kiss and a strong handshake. He was the proudest and happiest father in the world that day. But today, my dad is a different man and I cannot understand any of this at all. My dad, having remarried, has now distanced himself from my family and me. The man who was always there is hardly ever there. I guess, perhaps, that he misses me in ways that I know I will miss my children when they begin their journeys away from home. On those weekends with Dad, we would go to a soccer game, a bowling alley or scout function, but the best part was going to Movito's, a friendly little cafe only blocks from our house. Everyone knew us and we could shoot pool and play cards or video games. For Dad, in those divorce years, it was a place for us to be a family. Many times today in my mind's eye, I am sitting again in that back booth at Movito's, sketchpad in hand, rendering our times there. Those weekends would usually end with us clutching each other and sobbing as we said good-bye for another week.

Nothing More Need be Said

My Father

Christian Whitney

Why am I stuck in suppressed feelings? In all other respects I am a strong, independent person with a plan and direction. I have spent a lot of time dealing with this emptiness. I try to live a simple and honest life with some sort of meaning. My search for meaning has gone in many directions and I have found that the beauty of it all resides in my family. The other day my three-year-old son was helping me work on the car. It was life coming full circle. As we probed the engine and replaced parts, I found myself moving between the present as a father with his son and remembering similar times with my dad. Once I berated my son with sharp anger and stone silence; he responded by immediately grabbing me and holding tight. In that singular moment, my little son showed me that our connection, no matter what, was unbroken. Recently I invited Dad to his granddaughter's dance recital and I discovered I didn't want him to accept. I found myself trapped in a dilemma of confronting him over his emotional distancing from my family and me. His growing absence from our lives has caused a marked loss of intimacy. One day all of this culminated when my son, leaving his grandfather's arms, cried out, "Why don't you come to my house?" Thanks to my little son, I became totally aware that our family circle was unbroken. He did what I had been unable to do; he healed the lifelong wound divorcing me from myself and, ironically, from my dad. I am a father now and after all is said and done I am my own man as well. Welcome to our home Dad. Stop by and visit any time you can. Its really time we got together again.

Myself

The Obscure

Dad loved the obscure – obscure words and obscure facts. What was important about facts to him was that they should never be simple. They should always point the way to more facts, to more questions. I'll never forget how he taught me how to drive. We were circling the parking lot of the A & P as he explained to me the principles of inertia and motion, the laws of physics involved in starting and stopping a car. Of course, he mentioned Isaac Newton, probably threw in Archimedes as well. Fascinating facts but brakes seemed not to have been on his radar. We moved to the suburbs in 1949 and it seemed to make my father uneasy on one ground: religion. We were Jewish, unlike any of our immediate neighbors, and we chose a reformed temple in another town. When I went to college, I got a letter from him informing me now I could do what I wanted on the Jewish holidays (adding, nonetheless, that he himself always stayed away from work on those days). For him, attending synagogue was a way of standing up to be counted, and when people were counting, he wanted them to be sure to know he was a Jew. I went to services that year and have gone every year since.

He wanted me to excel in whatever I was doing and many years later, when, as a middle-aged woman, I attended law school, he asked me if I would make law review, reserved for only the best students. I told him he was putting a lot of pressure on me. "I've never meant to put pressure on you." He looked hurt and surprised. "I'm sorry," he said. The last time I saw him, in the hospital the day before he died at age ninety, I stood at the side of his bed holding his hand. "Do you remember, Daddy," I asked, "all those special adventures we had when I was little?" He had tubes and lines running all over and couldn't speak, but he looked up at me, his blue eyes twinkled and he squeezed my hand, just the way I had squeezed his when I was a child.

My Father

Rita Christopher

Since my father was a shy man, my mother was a social miracle, remembering names, faces, inquiring after family, always shining in conversation. Dad hid behind his facts. They shielded him from emotion, which made him uncomfortable. He had trouble saying thank you. Instead he always made a small joke by saying of every present, "Just what I always wanted." I've sometimes tried to use information in the same way. Often it is easier to make contact with another person by talking about a book or newspaper article than by talking about each other. When I feel particularly awkward, I find the easiest thing to do is to trot out some facts and do a performance, rather than having any conversation at all. It can seem friendly and engaging, but it is the way I learned from my father to keep emotion at arm's length. Somehow, I have also inherited his passion for perfection, or rather his intolerance of even the slightest mistake. When I began to play the flute, after he bought the instrument and paid for the teacher, my demonstrable mediocrity made him wince. In a similar way, I found myself demanding the impossible from my children. It has taken me a long time to think of a mistake as something to learn from. My father loved not only facts, but books; I loved the Saturday trips with him to the cluttered shop of Friedman the rare bookseller. Our living room was lined with bookshelves of my father's volumes. I can still see the titles, the long shelf filled with the green and red leather volumes of the Harvard Classics, Arthur Schlelsinger's Age of Jackson, Motley's The Rise of the Dutch Republic; and, like a reference librarian, whenever I asked a question, my father directed me to the proper book. When both my parents were dead, my sister and I were dismantling the house they had lived in for 50 years. We hesitated about the books; it seemed to both of us that selling them would be like selling my father's soul.

Myself

Un Fuerte Abrazo

Due to an early childhood event in which my father lost his patience, my juvenile defensive barricade was thrown up in our pathway of exchange. I couldn't allow myself to trust him up close anymore. Even though he would sit me on his knee and try to win me over, he could sense the fear underneath my frozen smile and knew that the possibility of our physical affection was significantly diminished. This emotional barricade remained until the age of twenty-three, when a gradual healing took place as I became a novice in the Order of Saint Dominic and joined in exchanging the brotherly Abrazo, the liturgical Kiss of Peace, in celebration of the Eucharist. As I write these lines, I now realize that it was in this sacred time of study and prayer that my juvenile barricade was dismantled. After the first few months of novitiate I made a visit home, and my father offered me his hand in greeting and, without hesitation, I gave him the Dominican Abrazo. Taken by surprise he stiffened in returning my embrace. On my next visit home, Dad greeted me at the door with a full Abrazo of love and peace. Joyously, the barricade was now gone and the circle completed. During subsequent visits, when I endeavored to explain how I came to believe that Divine Providence had guided me in the decision to join the Dominican Order, Dad interrupted me, saying that he had experienced similar guidance on his own path in life. This exchange encouraged me to ask both of my parents if they would be willing to write out their "life of faith." My mother gently declined, saying she felt it too personal to even attempt to write or speak about. My father responded with seven double-sided, handwritten pages. We had indeed entered the wider circle of the Divine Embrace.

My Father

It's said that ego is formed in a fearful response to some perceived threat. An ancient tradition teaches that this fortification occurs in the head, the heart or the gut, and borrowing traits from role models (parents), heroes and adversaries (anti-heroes), the personality then forms itself around this center. I believe that my Dad's nexus was not concentrated in his heart, but in the other two domains. At the height of the Vietnam War years, the military draft was reinstated, turning up the heat on all eligible categories. My response was to intensely debate my Dad on the merits of war, while seeking counsel in the writings of St. Augustine and other Christian thinkers. Finally, my priest and professor insisted that I "get off the fence" and submit my Conscientious Objector petition. Two signatures were required in verifying my veracity as a Conscientious Objector. My professor signed immediately and I approached my father to sign as well. Dad glanced at it and handed it back to me saying, "You know I disagree with you about all of this. Why would you think I'd sign it?" I replied, "Because you've roundly defeated me in every debate we've had on this issue, week after week. Who better would know that this is indeed a matter of conscience for me?" He then went into his study where he read the law. He returned, gesturing for the petition, signed it and handed it back. Within two weeks the notice came:

Status 1-0, Conscientious Objector. Another moment bringing great pain to our lives was when I chose to leave the Order of St. Dominic. My Dad especially suffered from this decision but he again elected to stand by me in an abrazio of fatherhood loyalty. To this day I draw on these "lessons of loyalty" and I continuously join in my Dad's practice of asking for the help of the Almighty in all of my affairs.

Dave Doherty

Myself

Lightning

Dad never swore or used the Lord's name in vain. He opened doors for women and stood up when one would approach the table. He was a pilot in the Army Air Force during World War II, assigned to the training of B-52 pilots, and practiced calisthenics practically every day of his life. But he let mom wear the pants in the family as they raised us with rigid discipline and threat of personal loss. We siblings sojourned through various levels of hell in an environment of too many rules and no freedom. Dad often sat through what we gals called "de-balling sessions" with mother, and when she was through he'd go upstairs with his tail between his legs and go to bed, but never before stopping and looking for a missing piece to his jigsaw puzzle that was always in place on the dining room table. I think it's easier for more men than women to adjust to the lack of intimacy. For them emotional distance is familiar, like a ghostly friend. My father lacked assertiveness and the will of confidence building. There was no flexible fathering to call upon (The only trip I took alone with him was to Chinatown when I was twelve and I felt like a princess). I was therefore compelled to seek my identity from others, which led to an immature marriage, a divorce and a frustrated search for a career. At the end of my father's life at age eighty-four, I visited him in the nursing home; his hands were trembling and when I asked if I could help him, he pointed to the medication that was supposed to give him an appetite and asked me to pour it in the sink. He was starving himself and wanted to let go. He said, "It is time." I asked dad why, when after mother died, I did not exist in his world after he remarried. He responded with utter silence.

My Father

Jane Fitzgerald

I look at the oak trees in the back yard; they are getting mad in the wind. The trunks are big and solid and fat, but the branches are slapping each other around like people sometimes do. For me, sadness has lost relevance and has become a narrowly defined pathology – whereas once, in a more exuberant century, there existed great gusts of oxygen inside the sadness. Sadness in that time was dignified; it was referred to as melancholy. It was a real affliction, like color blindness or flat feet. When I am angry I yell back. I can't hold a grudge and I don't believe in giving others the silent treatment. In my childhood, when the air was heavy and the skies darkened, great bolts of lightning cracked from the low hanging clouds, and thunder shook the ground. Mom worried that we kids might get hit by lightning but Dad never did; we would go out and play in the driving rain. We gasped over the most spectacular bolts, as if we were watching a fireworks show. Dad most assuredly left his stamp on me; the essentials of being neat and clean in appearance, ensuring that everything had a place and that everything was in its place. When I think of Dad, I recall him always clearing his throat before he spoke and I would immediately direct my attention to him, anxiously awaiting something that I could hold on to, something inspiring or validating. But there was only an awful sense of suppressed turbulence under the adamant order of things. It's very hard to argue from the absence of something. In reflecting now, I realize that being a mother has made me a better woman. I grew up with empty promises so it is essential that I be true to my word. I have become steeled by my father's segmented love; and, best of all, through my resiliency in that family carnival, I have grabbed the brass ring of a sharpened intuition. The central and driving force of my life now is to never suppress my dreams.

Myself

My father, John J. Murphy, was always known as "Murph." He was a firecracker of a man who contained an explosive, raging personality. Since I was the oldest of Murph's five sons and shared his name, I made it a point at a very young age to study this seemingly dangerous individual who, from the beginning, was the reference point for my existence. Murph was the son of Irish immigrants who treated life simply and warmly. They worked very hard and bore the philosophy of those hard times. Work was the mantra they lived by with family playing second fiddle. We lived around his work even though we had no clue what he did. When I asked him about it, he always said we'd talk about it another time. We had many conflicts. The final one took place when I dared to choose for my wife a girl who was not Irish. The night before my wedding was a tense one because I was becoming an individual on my own, owing to no one. Murph was wondering if I had lost my mind by not marrying an Irish girl. He sulked, but did the manly thing and congratulated me. Five months later, years of explosiveness, drinking, cigarettes and stress took Murph away one night at age forty-eight. (The supernova imploded on him and I was left deeply confused that the person I examined myself against was gone.) Three decades have fallen away since his death and I have gotten my act together. Several of my brothers carry psychological scars due to Murph's tough treatment and they cannot get past that anger, which is something I hate him for. But, today, I also love him for demonstrating to me that fatherhood is indeed an imperfect discipline, a discipline he had the guts to take on and stay with.

"Murph"

My Father

22

John Murphy, Jr.

As I enter the cooling off phases of the process, life has refined this impulsive lad into a man who bears testimony to Murph's legacy, but the imperfections are my own, as are my successes. I can be strong-willed or flexible, adept at dodging life's bad hops much as Murph dodged bad pitches as a high school athlete. The road I have taken is distinctly mine and I think Murph would have approved since he helped throw a few stones into the road to get me started. While I enjoy a very successful professional life, I have experienced a private life filled with all the ironies that a human can experience. Murph got into fatherhood in a big way being the scion of five sons; an option that I suspected would be reserved for me too. However, I have not experienced fatherhood at all because of my wife's brush with cancer. My life has been a study in nonconformity for those who have thought to have expectations "for" me. Those expectations could only be realized if I bought into the idea first; hence I am more like Murph than I ever thought. My adult personal life has been filled with tumult owing to my inability to be a consistently strong personality for my wife and her mother. Unfortunately there have been regrets due to missed opportunities in avoiding those little disasters (whether they be emotional, financial or matrimonial), which seem to befall us all when the emotional veto power is exercised. So I have to work a lot harder to repair the damages done. Like Murph I have put my energies into my work to ensure that the "damages" are taken care of, and despite the forces of life ever trying to pull the rug out from under us, I have maintained a strong internal core of values that I defy anyone to attempt to change. Though my circle may not be complete, thanks to Murph it is not a straight line headed for disaster.

Myself

Kissel Kar

My father fell in love with cars on the day his father picked him up from Ellis Island and put him in the backseat of a 1915 Kissel Kar. For the rest of his life, every car he owned, every Mercury, Lincoln, Thunderbird or Buick was cherished from its chrome bumpers to its bold hood ornaments. He was bitterly disappointed when I was not born the boy he felt he deserved and, worse, parenthood forced him to trade his snappy Ford coupe convertible for a stodgy, unglamorous Nash, outfitted with suicide doors. The day he brought mother and baby home from the hospital he carefully helped us out of the back seat and into the house. He then drove the car into the garage without closing its back door, ripping it clean off the car. Forevermore, he would refer to me as the "kid who wrecked my Nash." He judged me an endless, expensive disappointment with little resale value and would challenge my presence at the dinner table with "Tell me what you did today to justify my spending money to feed you!" His acknowledgement was always for sale, the price being my willingness to kneel next to a tire and, armed with a tiny pillow of steel wool, scrub away the flecks of tar that stained the hubcaps. Only then would he step back, nod with approval and say, "Good job, keep it up, kid." I would scavenge for attention he would not give and offered nothing he wanted in return. Eventually I abandoned hope. Our presence in each other's life was as futile as a car that circles a track without any expectation of reaching a destination. Fueled by anger and with no map to show us to reach one another, we lived until he died without knowing the road to a place where we might have believed we mattered to each other.

My Father

When my father died I was overcome with relief, as if I could finally breathe without his omnipresent disapproval. When I had lived with him, his was a persona of such loosely tethered anger and condemnation that it was prudent to recognize him as having only one dimension. If there were moments when he was less fearsome I knew it was because of a martini. Much as I wanted to, it was best to never lower my guard. Daily I was tempered in a blast furnace of verbal abuse and hammered into a steel of resolve to be tough, obliterating my sense of innate goodness. I did battle with everyone and everything; daring the world to go ahead, give me its best shot, all the while grieving for a lack of protection. It was only after I saw his coffin slip into its crypt that I chose to take that ragged power and learn to live comfortably in my own skin, unashamed and unapologetic for the gift of being woman. But sometimes I think beyond the struggles of the child that was me to the child who became my father. Each of us, separated by gender and generation, had endured a journey through desolate landscapes knowing only the fierce need to survive at any cost. Today, my heart aches for us both.

Catherine Conant

Myself

A Diligent Man

Born in 1893, Dad was a small, handsome man, who had been struck by lightning as a boy and left with a withered arm. He rarely spoke of himself or his work, and never complained or raised his hand in anger. His pleasures were reading, gardening and smoking his pipe. He appeared to be friendless. Precluded from the top ranks of the Civil Service by his modest beginnings and lack of university education, he was sublimating his frustration by ensuring that his sons were equipped to succeed. At home there was mutual tolerance, but little overt affection. Mother's ardent Protestantism took precedence over her humanity and Dad's enjoyment of such things as Vaudeville had been stifled. Physically, Mother and her seven siblings towered over my dad, always with a slightly condescending attitude. The tension between Dad and my uncles was palpable; when their talk turned to politics, he would stab at them with his pipe or retreat behind a cloud of smoke to recoup. Alone he relaxed, and I was always welcome to be with him as he worked in the garden or house, learning by osmosis. My more poignant memories begin in 1939, when WWII began and then, a few months later, when Dad and I stood watching London burn. I sensed his stoicism and knew there would be no panic. I went with my parents when his office was evacuated to a small town in North Wales. To my surprise he seemed to blossom in the new environment. With his colleagues and their families Dad was at ease and at the center of many pleasant social evenings. He took me on walks and bike rides, and his knowledge of plants was inexhaustible. I was reminded of those happy times when he retired in 1958 and received an honor from the new Queen for his service. After the ceremony, I watched with pleasure as he chatted and laughed with his peers, and my feelings of warm affinity were enhanced.

My Father

We start life by unconsciously absorbing the modus vivendi of our parents, unaware of any impermanence. I was surprised to learn after Dad's death that, as teenagers, my brothers had found him autocratic and distant; perhaps he still had been fighting his frustrations. Looking back, Dad's influence on me was benign and harder to define but certainly more powerful than my mother's. One exception was the pipe, which I rejected absolutely. For better or worse I inherited Dad's stoicism and ability to cope, a honed instinct to make the best of what is before seeking change. I also adopted Dad's socialism insofar as it rejected a disdain of people who presume superiority and privilege based on money, birth or religion. But I remember his wry chuckles when I tried to defend capitalism. His work had been investigating estate and company tax fraud, and he had lived through the Great Depression, the breaking of the general strike and two world wars. Besides shaping his politics, these experiences led him to value security. I wanted to be an actor, but Dad could not accept one of his sons in such an insecure profession. Did I give in because at heart I shared his fears? My life has been full and rewarding, but a nagging "what if" remains. He would have enjoyed the irony that my two sons chose to leave university before graduating, yet now run their own successful businesses. As in Dad's life, books and gardens have been important in mine. Together with family they provide a foil to a world increasingly irrational in its priorities. Because of our age difference and my career choice, Dad and I had few chances to come together. Like so many sons, I regret now not making an effort to close the gap. When his coffin slipped from view I felt his passing physically, realizing too late how much I owed him and how much of our relationship remained unfulfilled. Some forty years later, I now know much of what defines me is his legacy.

John Wells

Myself

My father loved me. He called me Chipmunk, my little Sweetheart, and when Germany invaded Poland, he called me Blitzkrieg. My father was tall, handsome and very bright. He had a Phi Beta Kappa key and I wondered why he wasn't president. He chose books for me to read, listened as I recited The Charge of the Light Brigade for school and helped me as I cried my way through Algebra. My father wore spats and took my mother to dinner parties in the middle of the week. He played the guitar and Aunt Fritzie sang Red Sails in the Sunset. I could hear them from the top of the stairs. My father loved opera. We listened to the baritone Lawrence Tibbett on Sundays. He said that Marion Anderson could never be great because black people could not stay consistently on key. My father was precise and strict. He cautioned me not to swear because it showed a lack of vocabulary. He never told me not to drink or smoke, but I never did because I was afraid of his disapproval. He smoked Lucky Strikes and drank cocktails. At the dinner table my father talked about world events, politics and business. At odds with what he said about Marion Anderson, race, religion or color was never mentioned in these conversations. My father took the train from Cincinnati to New York every week on business so I didn't see him very much, but we went bowling on the weekends and played Ping Pong, and listened to Amos and Andy. One day my father dropped dead. I was sixteen, he was forty-five. Years later, because of Marion Anderson, I wondered if I would consider him a racist in today's world and even more I began to wonder if I really knew him at all.

I Was Sixteen, He Was Forty-Five

My Father

Mary Stambaugh

Immediately after my father's death, my stoic mother retreated into widowhood. She was alone in a house that once bustled with family life. I was sent to town to buy her mourning clothes, black for winter, white for summer. Realizing my father's death was not a dream and remembering whenever he asked me to do something he used the phrase, "Carry your message to Garcia," I instinctively knew I had full responsibility to make up for his absence. World War II loomed and, together, mother and I along with everyone else worked for the Red Cross, the Ferry Command, the USO and hospitals. We sewed and knitted and bought War Bonds. In time, my mother remarried and I had a recurring dream that my father returned, and I had to choose between him and my stepfather. My father's family, going back many generations, was so fiercely Protestant in their faith that when, in father's younger years, he was asked to serve as a groomsman at a Catholic friend's wedding, his mother said she would disinherit him if he did. He rebelled and served in the wedding. It was to become his last appearance in church and it became the cornerstone to his character. The incident also served as my first encounter with intolerance. I am fortunate to have grown to old age without bias toward people and I regret that my father didn't live to hear Marion Anderson sing in front of the Lincoln Memorial. I know he would have agreed that she was very much on key. From the vantage point of these many years, I can see now that I learned more from my father's death than from his life. The legacy he instilled in me was a sense of loyalty, reliability and promptness – the exact tools one needs in successfully carrying a message to Garcia.

"It is not book-learning young men (and women) need, nor instruction about this and that, but a stiffening of the vertebrae which will cause them to be loyal to a trust, to act promptly, concentrate their energies: do the thing; "Carry a message to Garcia!" (Inspirational leaflet by Elbert Hubbard, "A Message to Garcia," 1889)

Myself

My father was a domineering, imposing man, a self-made businessman who worked twelve-hour days and spent very little time with his children. One exception was the annual hunting excursion, a day between Thanksgiving and Christmas, when I would accompany him for a numbing morning in the fields of rural Kansas. I dreaded the trips from an early age, when my role had been to struggle along behind him and his cousin Harold, ladened with a Pan Am flight bag stuffed with bloody quail and squirrels. The day after my father died in 1974, rolling his Chevy Blazer down an embankment after work one November evening, my mother asked my brother Jeff, my brother-in-law Mike and me to search the crash site for my father's pistol, his defense against robbers at his store. We walked the steep hillside in the cold for about an hour. As we decided to give up, I gave one final kick to some leaves, and there was the gun. Bending to pick it up, I noticed the white corner of a piece of paper a few inches away. It was my father's business card, speckled with blood. I gave the pistol to Mike and slipped the card into my pocket. I kept that card for fifteen years, until I was ready to throw it away.

The Hunt

My Father

Alan Pendleton

As the thirtieth anniversary of my father's death approaches, the anger and resentment I harbored against him for years have largely subsided, replaced with regret, sorrow, and compassion. He was only fifty-six years of age when he died, a scant three years older than I am today, and as I recall the days subsequent to his accident, I long to have known him as an adult, and even more, for him to have known me. I have no delusions that we would have been close friends; our interests were mismatched and our politics in polar opposition, yet perhaps we could have learned to get along, to accept our differences and appreciate our virtues. My father was a charitable man, with a talent for making people laugh, and an uncanny ability to charm strangers, put them at ease. Writing these words serves as a sort of confession, helping vanquish blame and guilt, carving out space for new, more mature feelings.

Myself

P ure-cognition in a time of extreme action; I have to this day an awesome and powerful trace of one of those fork-in-the-road moments in life. Once during my high school years, my father, a police officer, had loaned me his car with the absolute expectation that I would return and pick him up at the end of his tour, a sacred time for any cop: getting off duty. I was there on the dot; he motioned me from the driver's seat and in an oddly brutal manner positioned himself for full-acceleration in taking the road. Suddenly, a powerful awareness told me that a man was going to step in front of the car. I yelled, "STOP! A man is there!" Father, still in synch with his fierce energy, braked the car with such a force that we lunged into the windshield and, simultaneously, the man, with super-human strength, slammed his hands on the hood. His face, in agate-stare, locked into our very being. Oblivion held the air as in the deafening noise-dust at the apogee of a fatal accident. After an eternity, the man lifted his hands and quickly disappeared into the night. We drove home in silence. Father never acknowledged the reprieve-moment of certain death. I did. Somehow, the miracle of that moment had, for the first time, put me on par with my father, an emotionally distant, distant-man. But this story begins long before my time. It is part and parcel of the Irish Protestant Orange tribe, tight-lipped and defensive in every aspect of their character and, perhaps, it was even more a part of the bleak isolation of him being raised in the hard-ice of the North Woods of Minnesota, competing with twelve brothers and sisters, and of always-assigned chores of hard work with no nurturing of a sense of individual self, none, never, not at all.

"STOP! A Man is There!"

My Father

Jess Maghan

My childhood sense of survival was honed under the rubric of don't make waves and always take a secondary position in dealing with others. Over time this rubric imbedded in me a near fatal tendency for self-abnegation. It ultimately manifested as an exact duplication of the modus operandi employed by my father in his police officer personality. In many ways my father was a lone soldier his entire life; first during the Depression years of the 1930s and then during World War II, while serving as a police patrol officer in our nation's capitol after which he could not adjust to the confounding decades of social change, civil unrest and the race riots in the 1960s. I was haunted by his footsteps on the treadmill of his night patrols. They resounded in my ultimate choice of a career in law enforcement, doctoral research, teaching and writing about police and prison officers. Through these choices I have discovered that I also identify with my father through a veil of unclaimed pain. In an uncharacteristic moment my father once shared with me his desire to someday write a book of his police beat ruminations. But like a sparrow with a broken wing, his attempts to fly were both inspiring and awful. He would short-circuit his ideas by flaring into the inbred bitterness of his reified low self-esteem. By the time he joined the parade of walkers and wheelchairs, we had opted for a feigned father-and-son relationship of rearranging the porch furniture and never entering the house at all. While delivering the eulogy at his funeral, I let out the primal cry of a lost sheep.

Myself

Service Above Self

Dad was laconic by nature and virtually incapable of small talk. Having been brought up as a devout Methodist, he totally rejected any form of religion in his adult life. I don't think that he ever experienced joy or the ecstasy of physical love. My mother once confided to me that in forty years of marriage she and my father had only been intimate on six occasions. His reticence was such that it was virtually impossible for him to express emotions of any kind. I'm not so sure that he ever experienced deep sorrow or grief either. Although we were far from prosperous, his self-sacrifice was such that, in addition to my brother and me, my parents supported three young boys from the village through grammar school and university. We lived in the coal-mining village of Clowne in the Derby-Nottingham Coalfield in the north of England, where the mines were the only employer. Apart from the unhealthy fetid air, working conditions were both hazardous and hard. It was not unusual for miners to creep on all fours up to the coalface and then lying on their side, cut the coal from a seam. Dad was a physician conscientious beyond belief. Early in the 1950s, there was a catastrophic pit disaster in our village. All the miners from the morning shift were trapped underground along with the pit ponies. Dad did not sleep for three days, remaining on duty at the pit top to treat survivors as they were brought up in a cage. Father had two party tricks he loved to perform and which we children never tired of seeing. He would bounce on his backside like a rubber ball, often in time to music. His other trick was to blow smoke from his cigarette into his empty, upside-down boiled eggshell and then solemnly tap the top with his spoon and remove the top so that the smoke came floating out. I just loved that trick even though I knew it wasn't for real. Dad only told me once that he loved me and that was when he had been given the final morphine shot before his death.

Margot Knowles

With the exception of my husband, my father was the most highly principled person I have ever known. He taught me that you should never be involved in anything you felt was morally wrong. At one point in my professional life I elected to leave a medical project, as it was quite clearly exploiting the human condition, and I never looked back. Dad had no time for frivolity. He worked constantly and when not working, he was thinking about it. Unlike him, I am not a workaholic and mentally healthy as a result. A highlight of my youth was the one and only time I was top of the class. I knew Dad was thrilled but somehow couldn't express it. Family always took second place. At mealtime he insisted on a clean plate, reminding us that "the starving hoards of the world would be happy to devour any unconsumed food." He appreciated irony and had a lovely sense of humor. I recall Dad's amusement when John Paddy, a local miner's son, took chalk and wrote in crooked letters above the surgery door, "Abandon Hope All Ye Who Enter Here!" I thought Dad would be furious, but instead he guffawed, finding it hilarious. As a physician, Dad had a kind of magic about him that totally disarmed children and helped them overcome fear of needles and nasty-tasting medicines. I have blessedly inherited aspects of this behavior in my professional life. He led an admirably selfless life and his humanitarianism now anchors my life. Although for many years I deeply regretted he would not permit me to go to medical school, I succeeded in pursuing a career as a speech therapist practicing in Great Britain, South Africa and Sri Lanka. Working with virtually no resources at Little Woodford School for Deaf Children in Sri Lanka was where I feel I made the most impact. I continue to remind my own children how important it is to develop a sense of service above self in nurturing their ability to transform dreams into realities.

Myself

Though my father had provided the economic anchor for my college tuition, whenever I would show him prints of construction documents for a project I was working on he'd only say, "That's a lot of work." I felt that his disinterest in reading anything but the morning paper left him without the eye or vocabulary needed to discuss my work. But he never pretended to be other than himself, and there was pride in his voice when speaking of my education and ability. In looking through family albums now I see Dad as a dapper young man with wire-rimmed glasses, looking well-heeled and happy; Dad in shorts hiking on wooded slopes; Dad as a traveling salesman and Dad with cocktail in hand amidst smiling companions at various restaurants. I also see Dad as an old man with his walker by his side, bent over and steadying himself as he paints a side railing. That photograph shows him giving it his best, but in the end the arthritic pain grabbed all his attention and years of declining health continued to cast shadows until his death. The memories caught in these photographs now serve as the shell of our lives together. When he was in his fifties he and Mom built a lakeside house next to my grandfather's and shared it generously with their friends and relatives. To build a place you love for people you love is a remarkable legacy. The inheritance of Dad's cottage has now enabled me to have a new home of my own - no more words are required.

"That's a Lot of Work."

My Father

Stephen L. Lloyd

I have come to understand that the energy of the world works as the generations leapfrog each other, creating successive high points in spite of inherited infirmities and human mistakes. When Dad's mother died, we drove to the guesthouse where she had been staying and found her lifeless on her bed. Thirty-one years later I saw Dad on his own bed, lifeless, eyes open and filled with a look of anxiety. He had always been a remarkably intuitive man and even after he died I would "call on him" to help me find things I'd lost around my office. I'd ask out loud and, glancing to the side, my eyes would somehow fall on the missing object. Years later Dad's mysterious capacity again surrounded me when I finally found myself. It was during my civil union ceremony on a hilltop in Vermont where my partner and I had joyfully declared our shared bond and love before gathered friends and relatives. After the ceremony my aunt whispered to me, "Your parents would be proud of you." A buoyant feeling I had never known held my spirit. There were no obscuring shadows in the midday solstice sun. Immediately and without question I realized that the intuitive vein I had inherited from my Dad was now my very own.

Myself

Inborn Teacher

My father was born with scarlet fever in New York City and suffered close to death on several occasions. To help him gain his health, he was sent to live with a German family in Connecticut. It was made clear, however, that when my father reached the age of fifteen, he needed to get a job. My father headed straight to New York City and found work in the theatre. But the boy who did not finish high school was an avid reader and his spare time was spent haunting used bookstores, where he cultivated a lifelong love affair with books. The real turning point in his life came when he worked as the general manager for the Broadway hit, The Great Waltz, which was on its second national tour and where he met the love of his life, my mother. After forty-five years in the theater, at age sixty, my father was confronted with starting a new career in rural Connecticut. An old friend guided him to a job in the town library and this was destined to become his long-sought niche with his beloved books. He was almost twenty years older than my mother and about that same number of years older than the fathers of my classmates. He laid down curfew hours and dates were allowed weekend nights only. It was always a bit embarrassing to tell a date that my father required that I have the car and myself home by eleven. This made me pretty unsure of myself and I was leagues behind my classmates in the world of sexual adventures. Though I bristled under these rules, I somehow was comforted by them. Dad and I talked about everything but, strangely, never about what my high school sports meant to me. Yet, I still hold vivid memories of spotting him standing in the doorway of the gym at the end of several games, proudly watching me on the court.

My Father

38

My father had the dream but I fulfilled it. He would have done anything to finish high school and college and go on to become a teacher. I now realize that my father fantasized my life as much as I had fantasized him making his way across the country by rail and working in the early movie industry at Hollywood's Universal Studio, then later on Broadway. His world seemed totally glamorous to me, certainly more so than being a high school teacher. When the Superintendent of Schools announced my hiring, he noted that he now had a teacher with the second-greatest knowledge of history in town (acknowledging my father as having the most). While Fulbright Grants and teaching scholarships enabled me to travel the world, my experiences could never match Dad's book knowledge of world history. In his sixty-eighth year my father was able to tell me that he loved me, and as time passed it became abundantly clear that I was as much his hero as he was mine. Dad passed away five months before his eightieth birthday. To this day, I see him in virtually everything I do. He's there in every decision I make and every path I follow. I have married a keen and "book loving" teacher and whenever I pick up a book, usually history, I have a vision of Dad hovering over the pages of a favorite volume. My resentment of having a father several decades older than the fathers of my peers has long since evaporated, magnifying the inborn teacher in my life to be my Dad.

Keith Dauer

Myself

I didn't have a daddy. I had a father. And that was a different species altogether. Daddies wore shoes large enough for you to hide in; they stood in the doorway like unmoveable bulwarks when the overflow from the project's outside insanity flooded its banks and tried to push its way into the household. Having a daddy was greater than having money. Having a daddy meant you were a whole and entire person in the world, not a torn scrap of a person, or a remnant from some thrown-away relationship that no longer existed. In the world of my early childhood my father was a shadowy figure, close enough to watch but too far away to make any real impact. My father had a wife who was not my mother. He married this woman, an older lady, in order to remain in the United States. When I was old enough to understand that I was a "love child" who didn't merit her blood father's last name, my mother admitted to me that his love had been too much to resist, and she found herself loving him back. He was her rescuer and their love had a paternal quality; she was twenty-three and he was forty-eight. My mother described the agony of what it was like to be sitting on one side of a church with me, an infant in her arms, while my father sat on the other side with his older wife. So "daddy" came and went and never stayed for good. But he never came empty-handed, and he called my name with a fondness and possessiveness that no one to this day has matched. By the time I was sixteen, I still didn't know what to call him. I simply said, "Hey," and waved my hand when I wanted to get his attention. Somehow, seeing the two of them together, my father and my mother, it just didn't seem logical. She was a young woman driving about town with a man who was old enough to be her father. How could he be her father and mine too?

He Never Came Empty-Handed

My Father

I could not find him that day. I knew he was buried in a hand-me-down suit in another man's grave, and this grave would be forever unknown. Had this man I'd called father really existed? Who, beside me, actually cared that he had once lived? Why should it even matter anymore? His seed had helped to fashion me, to dictate who I was, and in the dust of all those days, I can finally acknowledge my birthright. Our blood is forever mingled and his life has been infused within mine. The remnants of his physical presence, his primitive features, have forced their way into my animated expressions and now reside in my face as they gently edge into the sleeping countenances of my children. Although I had initially discounted the material things he provided, I recognize his foresight in providing for my parochial school education, sparking the formidable will to see myself in college, in the mainstream world and beyond the borders of my housing project. Hadn't he engendered in me the ferocity to succeed on my own? I now understand those years of our ever-aborted connections was pure destiny. I need a history based on my own self-definitions. At my father's grave-spot that day, the Little-Girl-Cindy yearned to weep, but the Woman-Cindy could not. Not anymore. On that day in the cemetery I gave myself permission to grow up and to take off the mask, as I buried the miniature world of my father and me in the cold space beyond words, and at long last freed both of us to rest in the peace of knowing that our lives were destined to be wrapped in circumstances severing any capacity for authentic love.

Cindy Brown Austin

Cindy Brown Austin

Myself

Home Base

The memory of my father has no continuity. It is instead a collection of bits and pieces, much like a quilt with each square being complete unto itself. My first memory of my father was a Steiff cat he sent me from Germany. It had blue-grey fur and blue glass eyes and mewed when you squeezed it. Growing up in the Frog Hollow section of Hartford, Connecticut, my father was distant from my day-to-day activities. I did have a sense early on that my mom and dad were different from the parents of the other kids. There was a strain in their relationship that I did not understand at the time. His attention never trickled down to me or my sister other than through a sharp reprimand. Although physically he was average, his presence commanded a certain amount of respect, which I could sense from others in his company. When he entered a room the dynamics changed. He was a career Army man, and I remember a rack of service medals hanging on the wall of his and mom's bedroom. However, there was one time when he quite unexpectedly came to the park to watch us play baseball. I can still see him leaning against a tree smiling in his three-season jacket, his hands in his pockets. It was just a neighborhood game and after some encouragement, he actually agreed to play. He even pitched an inning and tagged one of the Christiansen boys out at first base. My dad could run. Until then I had seen him mostly as an impartial observer but at that moment, to the delight of everyone there, he was a man of action. He was in a good mood that day, and his dancing eyes and easy laugh were contagious. As we walked home, he put his hand on my shoulder and gave me some pointers on a proper batting stance. It was a great day. It was just me and my dad.

My Father

My father was not a part of my adult life. He left when I was twelve. Through the years there was little to no communication and then we lost touch. Though I thought of him often, I felt it was not my place, right or wrong, to seek him out. When I was forty-one, I was informed that he had suffered a stroke. He was living in Canada at that time on my grandmother's farm. I flew up, basically to say goodbye, as I knew that being in his advanced years he might not have much time. I talked to him about people we had known, small talk of who was doing what. I could see in his eyes that he wanted to reach out, but did not have the emotional faculties to do so, and now lacked the physical as well. I did not want to read further into it than that. I left him saying that in the spring we would go fishing and that I had a new rod and reel I wanted him to try out. He died a month later. On the plane coming home from his funeral, I went back to that one golden moment after the baseball game when we walked home as father and son. I slumped into a state of melancholy, not because of the sadness of the occasion, but because of the missed opportunities of never having had a dialogue as men and for the way our relationship had played out. We just never made it to home base.

Bob Van Keirsbilck

"Artischer Kinder"

Friday dinners were almost sacred in my family. My job was to set out the Sabbath things. I loved the deep crimson challah covering with its gold trim. My mother made it herself. On Saturdays, Dad made breakfast for himself and Mom. Hearing him puttering around the kitchen made me feel safe and secure. It was the same when I heard his loud snoring at night; I knew all was well. He let me help with crossword puzzles, and it was a thrill when I offered a clue and watched him write in my answer. His temper mellowed as he aged, but his worrying got worse. He owned his own company and worked hard to be honorable. But his sense of humor would vanish anytime the subject of Nazi Germany came up. He couldn't even watch Hogan's Heroes – "They make the Germans out to be funny and humorous. There was nothing funny or humorous about them." My dad wore his heart on his sleeve, and I always knew where he stood. He would keep silent but his emotions and thoughts showed plainly on his face and in his eyes. His brother had committed suicide. A dark cloud covered his eyes whenever the subject came up. It was one of the deepest tortures of Dad's life. During the last hours of his life, I watched as my brother's strong and long-fingered hands gently grazed over Dad's brow to sooth his passing out of his world of renal failure and heart disease. Though I wish I hadn't inherited Dad's quick temper and his migraine gene, I am glad I have his humor and his eyes. As a kid, Dad had a dog, an Airedale named Jung, and he loved that dog all his life. He would often smile at the memory and say, "Ein braver Kerl" (A good dog). Whenever we would ask Dad what he wanted for his birthday, he always gave the same answer: "Artischer Kinder" (obedient children). Even when we were grown, and he was a grandfather … the same response, always.

My Father

44

I wear my father's signet ring with its deeply grooved lines on my right hand. He wore it when he lived in Portugal in the 1930s and used it to secure official impressions on legal documents. After his death, I learned that my mother wore the ring while he was in the army during WWII. When in a quandary about making a decision, I touch this ring and wonder what my father would have done. He never had a chance to pursue his first career choice of becoming a doctor. His next best choice to provide for our growing family after WWII was selling and buying pharmaceuticals. Actually, when we kids got sick, he was a better "doctor" than a bona fide physician. In business his handshake was his word. I also had the journey of a derailed first choice to be an editor in a publishing house; I ended up with the next best choice of thirty years in sales for an academic press. In my career, I too rarely had a written contract with a customer; my handshake was my word. My father read in several languages and always had a book either on his lap or near his chair. I believe the day he could no longer read was the day he started wanting to die. His understanding of human nature was the thing I loved and admired most about him, especially his ability to recognize his own limitations. He was never afraid to say he didn't know something. When I don't know something, I also use this gift of intense curiosity and creativity. Father served in Army Intelligence in WWII. His dog tags bore the capital "H," even though he was not an actively observant Jew. He used to tell us he was either very brave or very stupid. I know exactly what he was – courageous – a man of his own convictions. In the days before physical ailments and age dictated his features, I loved to watch my father, deep in thought, smoking the Meerschaum pipe he bought in London on V-E Day. To this day, the scent of pipe tobacco conjures up warm and comforting feelings.

Janie Pittendreigh

Myself

He was a remote man. He seems to have loved me in his way, but once I was into puberty he had no idea how to talk to me. He wasn't unkind; just on a totally different wavelength. He told me nothing about life, about money, about sex. When I was sent down from Cambridge for having a young woman in my room, he was shattered. His dreams of a great academic career for me were in tatters. "If you felt like that, why didn't you find a nice whore?" It didn't occur to him that there was affection in the affair, or that he'd never given me the first idea of how to find a nice whore. I realized then that grown-ups were a different species, and communication was impossible. But all the same I expected him to be faultless. Every year he brought the family to London for a trip to the Zoo. One year he forgot the tickets. I was shocked that he should have failed to be perfect and felt terribly sorry for him. Then I became an actor and wrote a play. When I showed it to him, he said, "I can't stand these filthy sexual plays." I agreed, but thought he was talking about some semi-pornographic shows in London. He was actually talking about my play in which two young people fell in love and had an affair. Yet my father was a man who caused scandal by marrying his half niece, and was more or less ostracized by their parents for the rest of his life. My father, a passionate man, then, ready to take on society for the sake of love. But later he came to Scotland to see me act, and I think was quite proud of me.

"Why Didn't You Find a Nice Whore?"

My Father

James Brabazon

I was never consciously aware of reacting against my father's idea of parenting; it simply seemed to me irrelevant, nothing to do with real life. In real life my children were just human beings, friends to be enjoyed because we were a family. It could be that my being an actor made a difference. The people I worked with were by definition unconventional, and totally uninterested in social class. Both my wives were working in theatre and television when I met them and shared these attitudes. Convention and class were very important to my parents. If I had behaved in anyway like my father my fellow actors would have ridiculed me. But I don't think this is the whole story. I've met many other fathers, in many different professions, who had the same experience that I had. It seems that some mutation occurred in my generation, which simply swept away the old way of doing things. The old image of the paterfamilias, with the big chair at the head of the dining table and the special armchair in the sitting room, the undisputed regulator of the law, simply disappeared as though it had never been. Friendship with the family took the place of authoritarianism, common sense took the place of regulation, flexibility replaced rigid rules. An easy recognition of the place of sex in the world replaced the hypocrisy, which somehow labeled sex disgusting and yet sacred at the same time. In some ways and in some places this revolution may have gone too far, but in my own relationship with my children there is a genuine love, both with them and among them, that is a total contrast to my relationship with my father, and I cannot but think this is a very great improvement.

Myself

My father was a golden boy. Raised by a triad of strong women, his domineering mother and two older sisters, he sat on the pinnacle of their tireless efforts. A smart, handsome young man, he was the first in his family not only to graduate from high school but to attend college. Poor but with the fervor of his feminine support system, he left the northeast to attend Duke University. Appalled and embarrassed by the cruel racism of the south in the 1930s, he returned north after graduation to marry and raise a family. He longed to be a poet and captured my mother's heart with carefully chosen words and stunning good looks. His family life was detoured by WWII and the navy, where he earned a Purple Heart and was golden no more. Tarnished and bruised by Hitler's Europe he spent six months in Britain recuperating from his physical wounds, and the rest of his life in New York dodging his emotional ones. Alcohol flowed freely in the fifties and a repressed wife and two small daughters were no match for the dysfunction it fueled. I was never fearful of my father but disdained the disease I saw as weakness rather than alcoholism. He had a metal plate in his right arm from the war and would show me the scar. Once with repulsive pre-teen arrogance, I challenged him with two questions: What grade was I in and what was my teacher's name? I knew he hadn't a clue. I hounded him in front of my older sister and mother, who were horrified and awed by my persistent rage. He left the house silently for one of the bars he frequented. From that night on he was a sitting duck and I kept him in my sights. If I couldn't break the bottle I'd become it. My teen years were not pretty. Eventually my family of origin separated and all lived in different states, fractured but slowly healing. I was fortunate to spend sober time with my father before he died. There was no epiphany, no resolution but there was peace and quiet; not the silence of humiliation but that of human connection.

Golden Boy

My Father

I dream about my father often, examining the life I shared with him. He comes to me as a calming figure, wise and understanding. I have no doubt that was truly what he wanted to be. I didn't understand the depth of his psychological wounds. At times I see my self as a functional sign between two people of substance. (My father, my son > greater than); I'm the sign in the equation, a generation of women's work. My father as a child had three women to support him. As an adult he had three women to support. We were the mirror image of his family of origin; an exact duplication. The unwieldy top-heavy triad he tried to balance on one hand, like a Chinese plate twirler, while holding a bottle in the other. Although my father didn't add up, my son is the man my father wanted to be, and that is his gift to me. I feel myself in this space-time continuum as a progression, children, great and grand. That is my gift to his memory.

Lucinda Pinchot

Myself

My father was born in Lithuania in 1905 and came to the United States as an infant. He went to school until grade six and then, at age twelve, went to work in the coalmines of Eastern Pennsylvania. When the mines shut down in the 1920s, the family migrated to Hartford, Connecticut where he met and married my mother. My father's brothers and sisters were a volatile clan, all heavy drinkers, emotionally charged, very loud speaking - lots of crying and acrimony. My mother's side was a happy bunch, lots of laughing and singing, always helping each other. I was born in 1942, in a six-family tenement in the south end of Hartford. My mother was devotedly catholic; my father had an aversion to religion in general. I experienced both worlds but never felt a belonging to either. My childhood was subject to the pendulum swings of my father's moods, from acts of tenderness and love to very dark and brutal, alcoholic-laden aggressions. He was physical, rough and athletic. He told many stories of the beauty and benefits of the natural world. He was a liberal democrat and socialist and very independent as a thinker. My father seemed to believe that undergoing pain and suffering, or being treated roughly, was advantageous in developing strength and character. I grew to fear his unpredictability. Finally, in fear of her life, my mother left my father and they were never to see each other again. Alone and in desolation, my father took his own life at age seventy-one. I still think and dream about my father. I'm still trying to please him in every design project that I do. I've been gifted with his innate emotional energy, which has become a driving force in my creativity.

Untouched Primal Source

My Father

Peter Good

I've always been untrusting of ideas that come to me too easily. For me, this feeling was set in motion a long time ago and fed by the hardened lack of faith my father had in my abilities. It's so paradoxical when ideas come without conscious process and reveal a certain purity unencumbered by the burden of correctness. They bypass the obstacle of doing what seems right or appropriate and spring from an untouched primal source. I now realize that my quest to achieve unorthodox creative solutions also employs an equally hardened conviction for achieving competency and craft. I have been building this foundation brick by brick, and today I am much more respectful of intuition and spontaneity in my creative work. I sense that I am rising higher and higher and as I do, the darker memories of my youth have become more distant and insignificant. Memories of hurt now become part of a much larger mosaic instead of being embodied in tiny tiles of past times. Now, I draw solace from immediate details of my life. Yes, thoughts of my father continue to weave in and out of this scenario but they surface more as counterpoint. I still think of my father's left thumb which was discolored by a burn that happened before I was born. I still remember the shape of a chip in his front tooth and the smell of kerosene when he cleaned the paint from his hands after work. Occasionally, he would sing a hymn: What a Friend We Have in Jesus. My mother would sing the love song, Always. I experience generosity and love manifest in my sons as a purging of the anger and aggression that was ever-present in my childhood. Moreover, and most importantly, the shadows of my dad's suicide have faded away, freeing me of judgment and the need to "fix" anything or anyone at all.

Myself

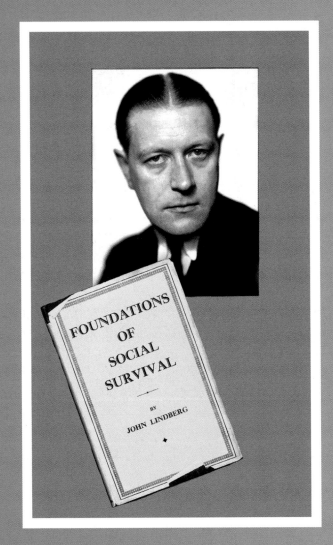

The more I knew him, the less I knew him. He had a genius I.Q. (I suffered from dyslexia and couldn't really read until I was thirteen.) He was blessed with a photographic memory and devoured one or more books a day. Underlying his arrogant, hardened veneer was the insecure and softer person to which he could not submit. At times he was receptive and warm, other days distant and coldly autocratic. I never knew what to expect emotionally and was scared by his many frequent extreme mood swings. Nonetheless, father was generous in letting me take part in grown-up conversations as long as I did not make a fool of myself or him; I was mainly to listen and learn. When I was about sixteen and father was a professor at the Institute for Advanced Studies in Princeton, many famous people of the day socialized at our house. After an occasion when T.S. Eliot, Arnold Toynbee and J. Robert Oppenheimer had been present, and during which I had dared to comment, father turned mockingly to me and said, "How can you know so much when you read so little?" This backhanded compliment was the first open recognition that I had mysteriously garnered an intellectual capacity. Father's high-stake power game ended in 1953 when he lost his candidacy for Secretary General of the United Nations to his colleague Dag Hammarskjold. It was a deep and traumatic wound to his ego but, in time, it changed his person and personality. Instead of exaggerating his aristocratic parentage and superiority, he finally let down his guard and surrendered his need to win in every situation or verbal contest. Over time he became humorous and caring – even an attentive listener. Having departed the arid temples of power and ego, he slipped into an inward state of calm grace. With his negative capacity exhausted, he found his true inner self to which he remained faithful until his death at seventy-six on the island of Majorca.

Halves Waiting to be Made Whole

My Father

Sam C. Lindberg

When I was eight and out for a rare walk alone with Father, I asked, "How much older are you than I am?" He playfully replied, "I am about five times as old as you are now. But in thirty years you will be half my age." A difficult concept for a dyslexic kid: Would I become half of what he is … what would that be? In 1940 we escaped wartime Europe and came to America where it was – and still is – axiomatic that each successive generation surpassed the preceding one. Contrary to this dictum, I fell short. In the mid-1960s, when I was in my mid-thirties and when New York City and the nation were undergoing profound social upheaval, I thought it opportune to dissolve my own publishing and consulting business. I sought a simpler life and moved to the country, where I bought a small and dying printing company, transforming it to profitability in two years, but a financing debacle with the Small Business Administration eventually forced me to close shop at a loss. With it went all my worldly goods and soon thereafter my wife as well. My wipe-out was total. Like Father, I learned humility. Fortunately, unlike Father, my defining crisis occurred early in mid-life. I could start anew in the work world and eventually in a new marriage of untold happiness. We are all halves waiting to be made whole. In this sense, living is when myth and reality merge, and truth is what is. Father's marriage was never happy. Emotional contentment eluded him. He sought recognition and authority. I sought a low profile, which allowed me freedom of action and thought secure in comfortable middle-class obscurity. Life and all happenings in it are random, including the dance of the ancestral genes. Each of us is created in our overlapping turns. Father never foretold that I might become older than he. What shall we measure other than I feel to be lesser than he?

Myself

Faceless and Enigmatic

I was born on April 24, 1944, in Hartford Hospital. Three months later my mother got on a bus and took me to a small town just outside of Hartford. She left me on the doorstep of a home belonging to a couple unknown to her. After that I became a ward of the state and was shuttled from foster home to foster home until I was adopted at the age of eight. The adjustment period to my new home was a difficult one as I was sure that some day the order "to pack your bags; you're leaving" would surely come. My adoptive parents were strict disciplinarians. I know that their intentions were good but at the time I found it overwhelming. As I grew older, I became obsessed with locating my biological father. I so craved a father figure that I created an imaginary one and kept it as a surrogate shield. Even as a small boy I wouldn't allow myself the luxury of forming a complete picture of what it would be like to find my biological father and get to know him. He remained faceless and enigmatic. I didn't know it then, but now I see that my imaginary father played a profound part in my growing up. He was an invisible prop that kept me from falling down. After a lifelong search, I finally located my mother in a nursing home and learned that my father's name was Rudy. I located his family only to learn that he had passed away a year before. Why a man would not want to know his own child is something I'll never understand, but unfortunately have learned to accept.

Adoptive Father

Biological Father

My Father

Dear Rudy: "I'm back!" Those two words were never heard by my mother or me. Psychologically I have been held hostage by you my entire life. Finally, after too many years, I'm able to reach around you and pull the rug out as you slide into a place I refuse to go. I have been retired now for two years after twenty years as a police officer and I have been married for thirty years. My wife and I are enjoying our new home. We have two children, a son and a daughter. Both are grown now and our lives revolve around each other in a way that keeps us close. I could go on about my life, Rudy, but you would probably shrug with indifference. So let me sum things up by saying … with the exception of a few bumps in the road, my life has been good.

You could have been a part of it but you chose not to be. I am sitting here smoking a cigar and enjoying the wildlife in our back yard. I blow a smoke ring; it rolls away from me then weakens, becomes distorted and then disappears. Tomorrow it will be just stale air. Get the message, Rudy! Here is a permanent good-bye from your son, the son you never knew.

Robert Buckland

Myself

With gray-blue, intelligent eyes that sparkled, Dad was never one to hug or touch much but was constantly there with his quiet deeply felt love for my mother, my two sisters and me, and I was always sure of his close supervision and protection. Somehow, I never felt childlike; I simply understood I should be polite to all ages and stay in the background. My father's first job was in a meat market. From there he went to work for the railroad. I have photographs of him as a skinny young man, standing with several grown men in front of their coal-fired engine. Even then Dad was ahead of his time in submitting patents for the train coal hoppers. Eventually, he became an engineer for a natural gas line, requiring our family to live at the site of an isolated pump station, where he was on duty 24-7. During World War II, we were under security conditions. I remember Dad as he sat watching the gas pressure gauges, where an unusual waver could signal a major leak or pipeline explosion, sighing and saying, "One of these days it is going to run out - then what?" In the winter we ice-skated on the two large artificial lakes that were built to cool the pump station engines. The gates to the station were chained and bolted at night and we had to sound a gong for one of Dad's men to let us in. Dad gave stern orders to his men and expected them to be followed, yet never berated or embarrassed them when a mistake was made. Over time I became aware of the utter dreariness of most people's lives in this remote region, and though I didn't realize then, I too was terribly lonesome. I would wave to the occasional Amish as they went by in horse-drawn buggies and wondered why they never waved back. How was it that in all that isolation, there was never any time for Dad and me to truly get to know each other?

"One of These Days it is Going to Run Out — Then What?"

My Father

When my husband told me his parents were not happy with our upcoming marriage, I said, "Well, for better or worse, we have to talk to them; bring it to a head, communicate." This capacity for stoicism in a moment of crisis is a direct gift from my father. For me, it is translated as holding my ground on what I think is ethically right and endeavoring to create an honorable result. The welfare of my five sons was of paramount importance, and the heartbreaks and hallelujahs of those days still echo in my heart. I was always there for them and like to think I worked really hard on their behalf. But the constant ache of seeking relief for my two bipolar sons, and in dealing with their breakdowns, has never matched my dreams for them to find the comfort of serenity. One can never fully repair the ongoing suffering and the losses for all of us, but time and again, I have leaned on memories of my father and his invaluable legacy of dependability, fidelity and determination, qualities also inherent to the skills needed in my lifelong work in the world of community service. I remember as a child that I would get strangely agitated when looking at the faded black and white photographs of my grandparents' log cabin. I wanted to hear the ghostly voices of the people in those pictures. I also have a vivid atavistic desire as I help to restore the home and memory of Charles Shepherd, a local hardworking, God-fearing, community father who lived in Springfield, Illinois. His diary (1878) tells me so much and, sensing a shadow at the kitchen window to be him I feel watched, and wonder as well if that shadow could possibly be my father. There is a feeling of gratitude that flows out of the house, encircling me with the simplicity and strength of the open prairies of pioneer times.

R-Lou Barker

Myself

Father Loved to Play the Violin

I hated him and I loved him; I despised him, yet I admired him. He taught me a great deal about life, by example and with words. He always had a cat-o'-nine-tails at hand, a razor strap or his quick-release belt, and the first thing I remember about him was that we got a whipping almost every day. When he was mad he would come at my brother or me; it didn't matter, as long as he got one of us. My father seemed to be trained to hate every other ethnic group, and he did so with gusto. He was, without a doubt, the most prejudiced man I have ever known. He was very handsome and he played first violin with the Hartford Symphony Orchestra. Some said he looked like the 1930s and '40s movie actor Fred MacMurray and, as a result, any woman was fair game, married or not. My mother divorced my father after twenty-five years of putting up with his amorous adventures, and in the end we lost our hundred-acre farm. My father had failed to make the mortgage payments. Grand Papa bought the mortgage and kicked my father, his own son, off the property and sold it. My father went off and married two more times. He had a stroke while married to his third wife, a German woman. She looked after him for a few years, then put him in bed and starved him to death. The death certificate said he had Alzheimer's disease, but I know he withdrew into that shell he was notorious for while married to my mother. He was seventy-five pounds at the time of his death and his beard was down to his chest. My father loved to play the violin and after he died, his third wife nailed it to the wall over his bed. She refused to give me his railroad watch and all I have now is the memory of the man I call my father.

My Father

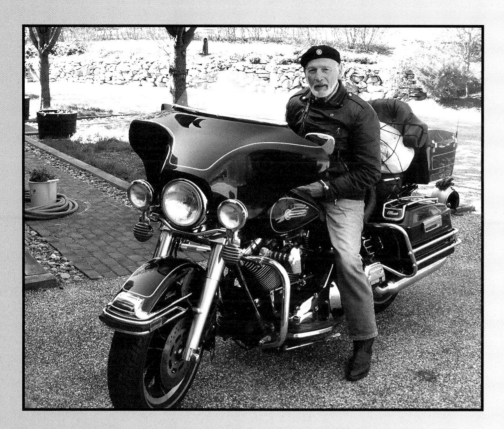

My father was a very "prejudging" man, but ironically my childhood experience prevented me from being prejudiced. As a child, I once got a beating for palling around with a Negro kid that I really liked. Now that I am the same age my father was when he died, I can say that he lives on, not only in me genetically, but in a sort of full life form. I look like him, I talk like him, and I even smell like he did in his later years. He declared early on that I would be a veterinarian; and at age sixty, after retiring from thirty years of teaching high school biology, I fulfilled his mandate in receiving my doctor of veterinary medicine degree. My father was a stern and forceful disciplinarian, but he made me into a better man than he was. Just before he died, my Aunt Ethyl took a picture of the skinny and bent-over old man he had become. The picture haunts me; I cannot look at it again. My father was no longer the big strong carpenter I knew, who could drive spikes into a two-by-four in the winter with his bare hands. Once while riding our horses across the back forty, a crow flew overhead and my Dad swung up the double-barreled shotgun, fired both barrels at once and almost knocked the horse to the ground. He could do any thing back then. He played violin. I play the harmonica. Mozart and Beethoven play within me. I am the wild horse running across the horizon and I am the eagle circling the sky. My father made me the person that I am today. I am the luckiest person in the world and don't even know it.

Lloyd D. Drager, Jr.

Myself

The Teachings of Silence

Dad had never had any qualms about killing fish and game for the table. It was a part of his upbringing that was being passed on to me. The first Monday after Thanksgiving found us in the Alleghany Mountains, overlooking a stand of white oak along Bear Creek. We sat among the hemlocks, which protected us from the falling snow. Dad handed me a sandwich without saying a word. It occurred to me that he never had much to say and he probably thought I talked too much. I watched as he slowly moved his head from side to side, scanning the creek bottom for a buck. In a slow, deliberate movement he raised his hand and pointed toward the bottom. Through the snow-laden trees I could plainly see a buck and two does standing in the shallow riffle, drinking, their backs covered with snow and fog-breath blowing from their nostrils. I had not yet killed my first deer, the sign of manhood to almost any young Pennsylvanian boy. I began to ease toward my rifle when Dad gently put his hand on my knee. He turned toward me with glistening hazel eyes, "Aren't they something?" We watched as they came into the oak stand, fed and moved off. I have filled my freezer with venison many times over, but that hunt, nearly forty years ago, is the best of my life. I've never spoken of that day with anyone, not even Dad. He never lectured. He just did the next right thing. He knew that the right thing to do that day was nothing. I'm convinced that at eighty-four he still hasn't a clue that he taught me so many valuable lessons through his silent example. He is still doing it today.

My Father

During the turmoil of my earlier adulthood I loved and hated my father for what I thought he was, while at the same time avoiding, with excess and selfishness, acceptance of the inevitable manifestation of father into son. A gesture of the hand, a yawn, the way I cross my legs; all gene driven and quite involuntary. That I was a quiet person with very little to say was but a pathetic way of pretending that I was a soulful thinker, like him. In reality I was only ignorant of life and lives around me, self indulgent and scared. In order to disguise my own inadequacies I demanded perfection of those around me and escaped into alcoholism when I didn't get it. I look at Dad now and realize that I never knew who he really was at all. With struggle, commitment and much help, I have cleared my mind. I have learned, through trial and error that no one is perfect and it is indeed our imperfections that make us who and what we are. I no longer place such demands on myself or others and am learning what it is to be human. People are much more interesting in themselves than I could ever make them in my mind. I used to love my Dad because he was my father. Now I love him because I know him. I am proud of my Dad and I can see in his eyes and in his grin, that he is proud of his son.

Mark Enie

Myself

My Father

My father's name was Cyprien; he had carrot-red hair. In 1913, when my mother was eighteen and I was born, my father was there and held me in his arms. After those first precious moments, I was destined never to be with him again. My father was in the very first battle of World War I at Charleroi, Belgium. It was the first German victory on the Western Front in 1914. My father was reported missing in action. His body was never found. Mother told me that he was "blown up by cannon." As a child, I fantasized that my father was the Unknown Soldier in the Arc de Triumph. On the night of the twenty-fifth of November 1920, when my half-sister Mimi was born, I was sent down to sleep on the couch in the living room. I was seven years old and feeling very much alone and down in the dumps on being put aside. Suddenly from behind a paravent in the far corner of the room, out stepped a vague shape. I knew it was my father. He came and stood looking down at me, and then, just as suddenly, he turned around and went back behind the screen. That's the only time I had ever really seen him and, yes, I knew it was he. Oh! I felt it then and ever since. It was my father. He didn't speak, but when he stood over me, I had a feeling of his strength. There is a certain way-of-being I have that comes directly from my father and now I realize it was in our blood. I did many of the same things he did. As a young man, he joined the French Army and went to Indochina. As a young woman, I joined the French Army and drove an ambulance during World War II, and, continuing in that spirit, at age seventy-five, I joined the United States Peace Corp and went to Guatemala.

Missing in Action

Eliane Marie Aubard Koeves

As a child when I was unhappy, I made Papa my refuge. I would pretend he had lost his memory, and that one day he would regain it and come back. In looking back on my childhood, I realize that my father grounded my being. Papa has always been my guidon. I've always seemed to know what to do in moments of danger. In many ways I am convinced that I am living the life that he would have lived, finishing the job so to speak. It is a rare privilege to be fulfilling a destiny. My father Cyprien was born 129 years ago and I know his indubitable and devilish spirit is in my sense of humor and adventure. I am my father after all. Merci, Papa cheri!

Myself

Despite crippling arthritis in his hands, persistent migraine headaches and eventually the loss of a leg, my father lived his life fully. He was a true economist, a most effective manager of scarce resources. Upon his own father's death, Dad's education ended in the seventh grade. He entered the work force at age eleven to help support his mother and ten older siblings. I can still hear his roar of laughter as he recited poetry and told stories after dinner, while we were all sitting around the dining room table. As a boy, walking with Dad, we would meet his friends who were veterans of WWI. There was Captain Walsh, who always walked ramrod straight, and Mr. Gerry, whom people in town referred to as "Dummy Gerry" because his speech was impossible to understand. Dad would always take time to chat with Mr. Gerry, having explained to me that he had been gassed in France during the war. One day, a lady who lived across the street yelled at us kids while were playing ball in the lot bordering her house. Dad's response was to be polite to her and to all ladies, and never talk back. Dad wasn't able to pay for my college studies, but along with the dictionary that I still use, he gave me a more valuable and sustaining gift, a contagious desire for learning. When I retired from a long career in banking, one question kept coming to mind; "How would Dad have handled this benchmark?" The answer was self-evident; Dad was always at home in the world with a definite satisfaction. While a senior in college, I sent a letter of gratitude to him and, now decades after his death, I wish I could do it again. I have no idea what his religious beliefs were. Evident to me, however, was Dad's awe of nature and his respect for all religions. I'll never know whether he made a spiritual connection from this, but as I ponder my religious beliefs today, I deeply regret that we never talked about it or God. Not once.

A Virtuous Man

My Father

Gerald J. Kelly

Dear Susan, Jerry, Eileen, Stephen: One day, years ago, I heard your Grandpa Kelly saying with pride that his children faced issues "straight in the eye." Even today, decades after he died, I am still supported by that confidence. My hope is that you are just as aware of my confidence in you. As you were growing up I tried to encourage your freedom of exploration without imposing my views, but one of the things I very much regret is never creating moments in the quiet of our home to discuss religious thoughts and beliefs. I wonder if Grandpa had a similar regret of not having talked about these things with me. He never had the benefit of adult conversations about such things with his own father who died when Grandpa was just a boy. Perhaps my silence was more that of a relatively young father, roughly your age today, who had not yet found solid religious convictions. Recently I was startled when hearing a reading that reminded fathers of the obligation to talk to their children about God: "And you shall love the Lord your God with all your heart and with all your being and with all your might. And these words that I charge you today shall be upon your heart. And you shall rehearse them to your children and speak them when you sit in your house and when you go on the way and when you lie down and when you rise. And you shall bind them as a sign on your hand and they shall be as circlets between your eyes. And you shall write them on the doorposts of your house and in your gates." (Deuteronomy: 4-7)

It sharply brought to mind an old concern about how my failure may have affected you. And it has persuaded me to now share with you a yearning for a spiritual aspect of our lives together which I will carry forever. Moreover, I share this yearning as an expression of my desire for your spiritual well-being and of my deeply felt love for you.

— Dad (Father's Day, 2007)

Myself

Forty-Eight

My father was a traveling salesman. On his frequent trips, he wrote loving letters to my older sister and brother, and me, and always reminded us of his motto: "One for All and All for One," from his favorite novel, The Three Musketeers. He loved baseball, especially the Yankees, and taught my brother Danny and me to play, always emphasizing fairness and teamwork. I remember that he shipped puppies home to us. The first one, a Toy Fox Terrier, came from Little Rock, Arkansas, and was appropriately named "Smokey." But he arrived sick with bloody diarrhea. I went to the kitchen early one morning and found him dead in his box. Then my father sent a bigger Fox Terrier we called Herman, who was a neighborhood character for more than fifteen years. But my father knew Herman for only one year. They said my father was rarely sick but on this last occasion he had come home with a ferocious earache. He got sicker and sicker, and was admitted to the hospital. Danny and I were in the backyard playing an imaginary ball game. We went inside and found a bunch of glum-looking people quietly hanging around. Danny asked, "Hi Mom; how's daddy?" She got up, and bravely carrying her awful burden, took us into our bedroom. My father was dead from meningitis. I was seven years old.

My Father

My remembrances of my father are almost all mental snapshots. His image has been created for me and by me from these few memories and the stories others told me. Have these memories and stories created me in his image. Is there fantasy, distortion, dishonesty? Who would I be if he'd lived another twenty or forty years? Isn't it a warning that you can't trust good stuff to stick around? Was some mystical power involved in my father's death at age forty-eight? His own father had died before he'd turned fifty. My big brother Danny lived in fear of not reaching his forty-ninth. We celebrated when he reached fifty. Then, at fifty-one, he was dead from a heart attack. So I, at age forty-eight, had to visit my mother late at night to tell her of Danny's death. My father's motto – "One for All and All for One" – was transformed into a coda for my kids: share fun and learn responsibility.

Phil Heilpern

When my kids were young I worried they'd be stricken by accident or grave illness and in some way this would be my fault. I realize that this was for me the father losing the child. But it's more than that. It's a belief I rarely allow myself to ponder (and have never shared). It's my sense that my life, in some predetermined way, has been the continuation of my father's; he is me and I am him. I was never too concerned about the forty-eight years syndrome striking me, because I know in my heart that Danny was sacrificed for both of us. Now I am seventy-four and whatever I reach is better than not reaching it at all. Is this a design? Is it luck? Perhaps! Luck may be the residue of design, but isn't it fate that determines design?

Myself

Lemonade Together

I am not sure I would have liked the man my mother married in the 1920s, a number of years before I was born. But the ostentatious taste, perhaps some arrogance, insouciance and other not uncommon trappings of wealth were totally diminished with the Great Depression and the ravages of World War II. I loved him deeply. Sixty-four years my senior, this love was mixed with awe and even some fear, and I still try to please him although he has been dead for more than fifty years. He was handsome, strong, athletic, had a beautiful voice and a wicked sense of humor. Despite the dramatic change in his economic status, he was always lord of the manor, no matter how humble the manor became and no matter how old and frail his body. His early life was a mystery, except for the anecdotes he regaled us with – of his being a runner for Cecil Rhodes in the 1890s where "the African moon was bright enough to read letters by" and of driving one of the first automobiles in

New York City. When meeting Henry Ford who suggested a business partnership, my father said to himself, "What! Mass-produce cars?" He never read me a story or taught me how to ride a bicycle, or told me about the books he was reading. But he did impress upon me the important things in life: honesty, integrity and doing your best; and, most of all, the big-little things like the necessity of doing calisthenics every morning and appreciating a good glass of wine or the delicate beauty of a flower. Even with an eighty-year-old, post-stroke and post-heart attack body, Father, when walking in the countryside after a rain, would always bend over to clear the rubble that clogged the way. Today I find myself comforted, as he did, in freeing storm drains of sticks and stones.

My Father

Nikki de Langley

Growing up, I took my father's demonstrative affection and love for granted, until I recognized it as a gift of immeasurable dimension that is shared in my household today. And though the occasional visitor appeared to bask in his sophisticated insight into world affairs, I was enriched by what lay beneath the Victorian veneer. His sensuality seeps through every pore and fiber of my body, as does his playfulness. Tears come to my eyes today when I hear beautiful music. Once when I was eight years old and he was seventy-two, my father had to pick me up from boarding school because my mother was in the hospital. Unsure of what to do with me, he took me to his old haunt, the Casino in Cannes, where we had lemonade. When we took the first sip of our lemonades, our lips pursed and our eyes shut tight. They were so sour! (It was the middle of World War II; there was no sugar to be had.) We continued to make funny faces at each other. This dignified Englishman giggled silently with me and we maintained decorum until our glasses were empty. I had met the child in my father. Years later I remember his old hand shaking as he pondered a piece of my mother's jewelry that could be sold to pay for my college tuition. When his body and health were failing, his grace, dignity and the twinkle in his eyes remained. That twinkle is ever here in my children and grandchildren. Laughter was the great equalizer, and always succeeded in shrinking the sixty-four years between us, as it does between my grandchildren and me. I often have to repress the utter joy and inner laughter I now feel in concert with my grandchildren, when they are doing something funny, but silly enough, to incur their mother's wrath – and it all began with very sour lemonade!

Myself

Fourth of July Fireworks

When I joined the Army in 1969, Mom and Dad took me to the train station. The good-byes from Mom were blubbery, but Dad held steady. When the train pulled away, however, I could see the tears welling up in his eyes, tears no doubt reflecting his memories of WWII. I have a black and white photo of a twenty-seven-year-old Dad right after he got out of the army. He's holding me and grinning. He looks very dapper in his brown fedora, light tweed blazer and dark slacks. I also have a photo of Dad taken in England at Piccadilly Circus just before the D-Day invasion, showing a boyish twenty-three-year-old with a confident air, his uniform displaying sergeant stripes and medals, plus the 29th Infantry Division patch. Later in life, Dad would always say, "I'm patriotic but I hate Fourth of July fireworks." This was to always be his unfortunate holiday and he dreaded its arrival. One Christmas, I got a replica of a real rifle and Dad gave me practice in military drilling: "Left Shoulder, Right Shoulder, Stand at Ease, Parade Rest!" On the sixtieth Anniversary of D-Day, my sisters and I accompanied Dad back to Omaha Beach.

Mom had died two years before and Dad was still struggling with the loss; and, for the first time, the focus was totally away from her and only on him. His tears had started to flow at the first sight of the water. He walked ahead of us as if pulled forward by an invisible force, quicker and quicker, until he felt he had reached the right location. "This is where I landed and that's the Nazi bunker at which I fired my first shot!" It was heart-wrenching to see him standing there awash in the bitter memories of that bloodied sand. Growing up, I was always puzzled why Dad never came to church with us. When I asked about his relationship with God, I can't recall him saying anything discouraging, only that "it might take time."

My Father

Vaughn Peterson

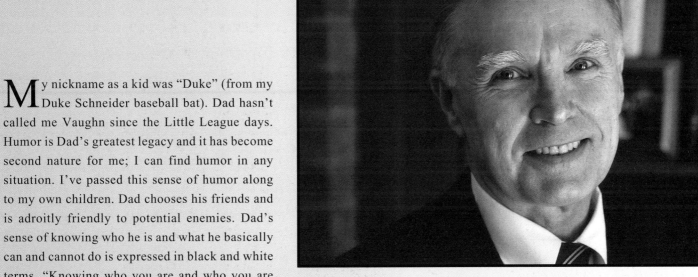

My nickname as a kid was "Duke" (from my Duke Schneider baseball bat). Dad hasn't called me Vaughn since the Little League days. Humor is Dad's greatest legacy and it has become second nature for me; I can find humor in any situation. I've passed this sense of humor along to my own children. Dad chooses his friends and is adroitly friendly to potential enemies. Dad's sense of knowing who he is and what he basically can and cannot do is expressed in black and white terms. "Knowing who you are and who you are not allows you to do anything." He is comfortable in his own skin and I am learning more and more to be that same way. I approach personal and professional situations with a logic that breaks things down to simpler forms and more manageable tasks. I follow sequential steps but I'll break schedule anytime for lunch with Dad. He opens up more often now and, as he describes it, "I can't say I've been happy since Mom died, but I'm content." I sense his deeply held survivor's guilt just below the surface: "I still don't know how I was able to survive D-Day." I am starting to think like him now. The assumed trappings of education and intellectualizing, status and material pressures no longer cloud my communication. By passing along Dad's simple clarities, I am helping my son develop his own philosophy of life.

Myself

My father was a Protestant pastor who ministered in Baptist churches for half a century, primarily in Appalachia. It is almost impossible to describe him without using the religious language in which he was saturated by culture and profession, yet he never succumbed to the plentiful humbug with which his profession was rife, especially in the Bible Belt. Instead he steadfastly refused to bow to the blandishments of institutional religion that bade him to compromise in order to gain preferment. He possessed something of a universal spirit. There is more to a man than his profession, even if it governs fifty years of his life. Born in a log cabin on the very pinnacle of the continental divide in the Blue Ridge Mountains of Virginia, and moving as a child with his family in a covered buckboard wagon, he lived long enough to travel the world by jet plane. Growing up in the rough mining camps of West Virginia, he began to drink, fight, and carry a pistol and bottle of moonshine whiskey. Recognizing his need to change, he gave up on moral rearmament and let himself be cleaned up through an encounter with divine grace as found in the Gospel of Matthew, Chapter six, verse 33, "Seek ye first the Kingdom of God … and all these things shall be added unto thee." As a pastor, his specialty was teaching people how to live, as well as how to be prepared to die. His natural talents became evident while still in his twenties, when he began to preach in churches in various coal-mining camps. As for his demise, one might say that there is no such thing as a successful death. But his death was my father's crowning achievement. Diagnosed at age eighty-three with congestive heart failure, he refused surgery. "No," he said, exhibiting great faith, "The Lord is in charge of how long I'll live. I think I'll just leave it up to him."

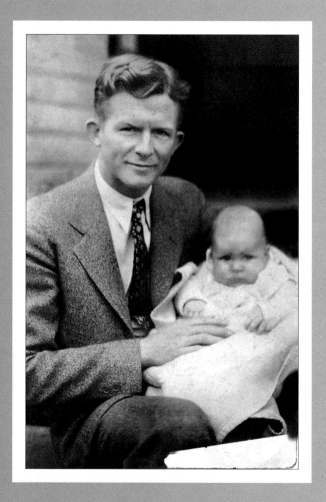

My Father

"Let Thy Mantle Fall on Me!"

With blessed continuity my father's spirit still reaches out to instruct me. Sometimes when engaged in mundane tasks or moments of high achievement, I get a glimpse like summer lightning of his shadow over my shoulder. Such strange manifestations are rare, and holding on to them is like trying to grasp quicksilver. He then seems the embodiment of an inner voice, pushing me forward, whispering in my ear, "Abjure financial allurement and mere honors; run away from anything that does not adhere to the truth; listen to your conscience; see the humanity in everyone you meet." He once took my hand as a boy and led me into a hobo camp down by the railroad. "These men need our help." Years later, I still feel those words subconsciously pushing me forward as I hand out food, blankets and medicine to refugees in Afghanistan, Iraq, the Sudan, Pakistan, Indonesia and many other places. At his funeral, I laid my hand on his and cried, "Father! Father! Let thy mantle fall on me!" Little did I know what I was asking? His mantle of selflessness, sincerity, service to others and purity of heart has become the spiritual capstone of all my life. Perhaps that's why I have not been afraid to condemn abuses of power and speak unpopular truths, whether in Baghdad, Moscow or Washington. The ancient Romans placed busts of their ancestors at the entrance of their homes as a way of invoking their ancestral identity. Today's faded photographs of older generations seem but a pale reflection of their intense practicality, affirming the most important thing in life – the historical trajectory affecting our destinies.

Jim Jennings

Myself

Woof Runs at Right Angles to the Warp

My father Henry "Hank" Miller was born in 1916, the youngest of six brothers to immigrant parents from Kovno, Russia. This young family, essentially matriarchal after their father's fatal heart attack, was a hardscrabble lot with the boys sleeping three to a bed. My father wanted out at an early age. His brother Dave rode him on the handlebars of his bike to hawk peanuts at the Yale Bowl where Dad, dazzled by the swanky cars and elegant clothes of the rich, got his first taste for luxury. He sensed the air of privilege they breathed but it was a quantity he barely understood. Nonetheless, this became his life's ambition though his journey was painfully interrupted at age twelve. Having no money for a boxing ticket, Dad climbed to the New Haven Arena roof. While watching the match, he fell ninety-five feet through an air shaft to his presumed death. Broken but alive, he spent a year in the hospital. He missed his Bar Mitzvah and was never able to recall the words he half-heartedly learned in

My Father

Hebrew school. Dad quit high school and at sixteen took a job at a custom tailoring shop. A few years later he married my Protestant mother and went into the army near the end of WWII. He then set out to earn money the only way he knew: driving the prep school and college circuit and selling clothing from his car's trunk. From this start, he became a haberdasher, primarily to the WASP community, which he also chose for his growing family. He was passionate about his English tweeds and fine cashmere. His tools were the tape measure, soap for crosshatch markings and long dressmaker pins he'd hold in his teeth. A handsome suit was always in the works. When a customer stood in the three-way mirror looking particularly splendid, Dad ran his hands over the material, unable to resist the cloth. They were his riches.

Today when I button a silk blouse or tie a soft knot in a challis scarf my fingers are entwined with his. We have the same hands, small, kind of stumpy with arthritis at the knuckles. Men are embarrassed when I run my hand over the stitching of their lapels or linger too long at a shoulder of a cashmere jacket. Reflections come back at me from a memory cave whenever these senses are at play. It's strange that although my mother has been dead for almost forty years, her death brought Dad into view. Now, as an adult past middle age, I sense my task at hand. This is the task, I believe, of authenticity and feeling comfortable with myself in this skin. I was prepared to judge my father harshly but found instead that he was simply a man who, because he was driven, made a better life for his family than his parents could make for him. I thought he owed me a Jewish heritage until this mysterious quantity, which inversely paralleled his own, unraveled over the year-and-a-half I studied for my conversion to Judaism and my Bat Mitzvah at age sixty-two. I did not make a mistake that day as I read from the Torah and welcomed the forefathers and mothers of my ancestry into my heart. I often imagine Dad delighted by it all and remember, too, the pirouettes in new dresses and his smiles of approval. I always knew my sense of style was his gift to me, but I never thought my love and wonderment of words came from him. Each time I struggle to stitch together the right words in a poem, I remember him showing me how the woof runs at right angles to the warp thread, embellishing the richness of texture and I try hard to evoke that intensity of his spirit in my own life and work.

Sue Levine

Myself

My father (my spiritual mentor) was born Isidoro Torres Pilapil and his image as an ideal son shone far above his six siblings. His parents had nothing but praises for him. He died at age twenty-six, defending his Philippine homeland from the Japanese invaders during World War II. My brief four years with him remain as picture-perfect memories. There is one of him atop a Tamarind tree situated by the edge of a creek, gathering young shoots while my mother and I wait below. Then there is a classic view of him walking with me in tow and my little brother riding on his shoulders. My last recollection of my father was when he came home dressed in his army uniform on a brief leave from the war to bury his son, my brother, who died of an infection; I was looking up, not understanding the meaning of the event, as he pushed the small coffin into an elevated niche. Many times, I would ask myself, "Why didn't my father come home when the war was over like many soldiers did? Why did he have to be a hero?" Today, as I look at my eighty-nine-year-old mother, I sense the unending loss she has suffered. I regret that other than a copy of a photograph of my father, I have no personal mementos. Often I "talk" to him. One special dialogue occurred when I graduated from medical school and I imagined announcing to him, "Dad, I am happy to tell you that your son is now a doctor." And when I had each of my children I would do the same, proudly telling him that he was a grandfather. I still ask my mother things I have asked many times before, and she is always happy to recall the stories of their life together. It seems I continuously rehearse the past, reliving it in my own memory, like reading a favorite old book over and over again with even more refreshed interest.

My Father

Doro

Gil Pilapil

Growing up, I had a pervasive feeling of humility in my relations with people. As a young boy, I kept our yard clean and trim without being told, raised a vegetable garden in our backyard and planted flowers along the walkway to our front door. One quality that has frequently been ascribed to my father was his sense of responsibility as a son, a husband and a father. Just hearing it seemed to convert that quality into my own sense of attitude and thinking; it became a natural part of me. When I was an intern at a university hospital where a seriously ill infant needed close monitoring one night, a strong sense of responsibility made me sit by that baby through the night until the crisis was over. In this regard, I have always felt safe and at home with the less fortunate. I have gone on numerous medical missions, donated medical equipment to hospitals and books to libraries, and initiated scholarships. The respect and deference I have for my grandmother reminds me of the way my father related to her. Because of the softness in the quality of the way grandmother treated us, it was as if I, too, were her little boy and I would behave as I perceived she felt, yielding to her evident satisfaction in holding and rubbing my arms. It is interesting that, for someone who as a youth was quick to express anger, I have matured into tempering my emotions during trying situations. If my father were alive today, I can imagine him being steadfast in his beliefs while remaining capable of compromise when needed. Those were traits I inherited from him and somehow leaned on while moving from one culture to another. My father will always live deeply in me, as I like to think that during our time together, I lived deeply in him.

"Keep on Jogging"

My Father

My father is a complex yet simple man. He walks around with only a few dollars in his pocket because the only thing he ever buys for himself is breakfast. He loves to run and has for as long as I can remember. He runs about three miles, three days a week and never varies his route. Once for his birthday, when I was thirteen, I made him a leather visor and stamped "Keep on Jogging" on its brim. My father is very impatient. In fact, he frequently interrupts people when they are speaking. But, for the important discussions, when a daughter is seeking advice in figuring out her life, for instance, he listens and offers his pragmatic wisdom. Once when I was in the hospital with a severe attack of Bell's palsy and could not move the muscles in my face, my father sat calmly at my bedside. I asked him if he thought I was going to be like this forever. His response was fast and direct. "Caryn, your whole life is in your head. You and only you can decide how well you are going to live it." The only thing I ever saw my father buy for himself was a small rectangular plaque that read, "Enjoy what you are!" He is able to let things go, which is why he doesn't suffer or play mind games with himself. As an assistant principal at a junior high school, he was the one who disciplined the "bad" kids and doled out detention or suspension. He never misused his power or took away the students' dignity when disciplining them. They understood and accepted their punishment. He also was in charge of making the schedule for the entire school. He loved this process because it was methodical and logical. He is a really good father and I love him dearly. He is liberal and open-minded. After my parents divorced when I was six, I lived with mother until age fifteen, and then I moved in with my father. I could sense that he made a conscious decision not to criticize me; I was home at last.

Every Saturday as he returned from a good breakfast with his friends, his grey Chevy Impala rounded the curve with my father smiling. Saturday was his favorite day, a winding down from another week of navigating frustrated kids afloat in the sea of public education. There's not an inkling of fatigue or burnout in his face and, as usual, he was ready to reinforce the best in me. He steered me away from focusing on life's impossibilities and gave me the freedom to become who and what I wanted to be, both personally and professionally. Mind reader, magician, pragmatist and clown, he'd vanquish the fear I had amassed during the past week from living with my mother, wipe the slate clean, and patiently restore my sense of self which became the foundation from which I was able to realize my dream of being a photographer. He would infuse this head-set in a matter of seconds, with quick eye contact and without

Caryn Davis

words; somehow his presence sparked pure confidence. Now, I understand his diligence in giving me all those Saturdays that I needed to master change, to dare to go out on my own. Like my father, I'm at home when I'm alone. He taught me that living with impatience will actually create the patience required in achieving a goal. His "what you see is what you get" attitude has now become the one consistent thread in my photographic work. My approach is to capture my subject in an honest manner that gives some insight into its true nature. This is the perfection of photography, a continuity of impatience-patience, the split-second lens of life. On this ticket, I was able to walk away from a lucrative corporate job and dive into the cold blue future, and like my father, I'll "keep on jogging." Most of all, I will know when to stop and recharge myself with the spiritual strength of Saturdays with Lenny – my father, my friend.

Myself

Gustaf Elmer Lindskog's ticket out of the Swedish ghetto in Roxbury, Massachusetts, was intellectual giftedness bordering on genius, combined with classic Scandinavian manual dexterity. His destination in surgery and medical research was groundbreaking exploration of the chest cavity and the first use of chemotherapy. His was the life of the mind, applied without hidden agendas or political intrigue. Home from the hospital at 5 p.m., my father would work on his textbook in thoracic surgery for an hour. Dinner in this professorial environment was called for 6 p.m. Seated at the head of the table, he would ask, "Did you play soccer today?" "Yes," we answered. "Did you win?" "Yes." "Did you score?" "Yes." Silence. As Ma served desert at 6:20, he would ask the same questions again, revealing the charade of his personal attentiveness. His textbook appeared in four editions. Even on annual August vacations on Great East Lake in New Hampshire, we were drilled in the details of swimming and fishing for small-mouthed bass, and accompanied him for the mandatory early morning dip. In his retirement he devoted himself to absorbing and lecturing on the history of medicine. His personification of the Geheimrat tradition never altered. Evenings, in his dotage and living in an in-law apartment in my home, he would shuffle in and, having forgotten his own intolerance of such intrusions, launch his conversational overture. Weary from ample, interpersonal activity during the day, I would flick the volume on the TV higher and higher. My wife and friends, like most of our generation intimidated into being their parents' children in perpetuity, chastised me for this reaction. My father died in 2002 at the age of ninety-nine. On my son's first day as assistant professor of orthopaedic surgery at Yale, his new patient inquired: "Are you any relation to the Dr. Lindskog?" "Yes," he replied. She smiled in response. "Your grandfather operated on me fifty years ago!"

Pioneer Surgeon

My Father

80

My own ticket was punched for financial independence, with a long detour to the final destination: personal validation. I started working at odd jobs at age eleven. At age twenty-one, I remember waking my father, who had returned from the hospital and fallen asleep on the sofa during the Texaco Opera broadcast, to tell him I had become engaged. His only response: "I hope you can afford it. Don't expect any financial help from me." In fact, I had not expected any. I was angered by the total lack of his personal endorsement that accompanied this encounter. Even though I knew that easy approval would have been granted for a career in surgery (however, without his financial participation), I had no interest. I identified and pursued a successful career in trust banking. In his last fifteen years, our relationship changed. Though earlier he had at times sought my financial advice, seeking ideas had progressed to adopting my recommendations. Living in our in-law apartment, he became increasingly frail. If he fell during the night, he would wait until sunrise and pound on the floor to alert me to his predicament. I would then lift him back onto the bed and confirm that there were no injuries. It felt strange that he was increasingly so dependent on me. He never acknowledged how he felt now that the tables were so totally turned. Perhaps the emotional distance between us pained him. I had dismissed that pain. My troubled, silent search for his validation had been alleviated by his longevity. I was able to accept the reality that his life was surgery, his manner clinically distant, and that I was an ancillary entity. My anger has abated, and I speak openly with pride of his accomplishments. I am pleased that my children knew him and were shaped by the same force. Now my grandchildren, warmed by my kisses, embraces and endorsements, are exploring the limits to which their gifts will take them.

Carl Lindskog

Myself

Afterword

Having spent thirty years in police and prison bureaucracies and fifteen years in academia, I have acquired a healthy respect for the power of authority. As training director for the New York City Department of Police, I worked directly with the most naked forms of authority and, as an international prisons consultant, I have studied it in depth and written about it extensively. And, inevitably perhaps, I have now turned my eye on the most iconic of all authority figures: fathers.

For this book, I invited people from totally diverse backgrounds to reflect upon the man who has the most profound impact on our lives: father. Whether he succeeded in his role as parent and provider, performed haphazardly or failed utterly in his traditional duties, the father of every person in this book returned to life as a force to be reckoned with and – more often than not – to be loved.

I suggest that everyone try this exercise: Take the pulse of a cross section of ordinary people by asking them about their fathers. When you do, you will be greeted by a smile, a frown or a contemplative stare into nowhere, but I promise you that almost all of them will respond with an astonishing interest. And you will also discover that each person, including those orphaned, abandoned or victimized by divorces, will reveal the universal desire we all have to be connected spiritually to the man we call "Father."

"IF YOU WANT TO UNDERSTAND SOMETHING,
TRY TO CHANGE IT."

—KERT LEWIN

The Creators

Jess Maghan

Author/Editor

The idea of this book comes from a lifelong and abiding interest in the intergenerational influences on character, choice of occupation and social identity. This book was also strongly influenced by thirty years of government service as a training administrator in police and prisons, and fifteen years as a professor of ethics and social justice, journalist and essayist.

Sam C. Lindberg

Photographer

Thirty years as a printing executive by definition meant a career of reproducing the works of others. This was so whether imaging Irving Penn fashion tableaus, presenting the Nelson Rockefeller Collection, printing art books and museum catalogs for Yale University or annual reports for Fortune 500corporations. His photography has moved from enabler to originator. The focus is people, concentrating on catching their mood, look and essence without varnish. He shows his subjects for who they are, as they are.

What is Force Field Writing?

This unique writing method is based on the work of social psychologist Dr. Kurt Lewin and his technique of placing individual "life spaces" (family, work, education) into a subjected forced field of definition. This mode of writing pulls together a virtual access for developing skills in writing venues within memoirs and biographies; fiction and nonfiction; poems and meditations, and a deftness at journaling.

In handling the past and present frames of life, you must first realize that your father had a father – a loving father or a father 'who was never there.' It is in the courage of letting go that releases a deadlock attitude blanketing it all. The first step is to be still and to welcome the insight of what is not being said in what is being said. Know the past and the present are constantly folding thin layers of the future and sifting them into your character and life.

For example, memory is an artful dodger and in many ways a psychic shield. Therefore, the informed writer becomes capable of having a singular creative baton in all aspects of life. One can see how drawing together insights from topology (life space), psychology (need, aspiration), and sociology (motive and pressure) aid in accurately recalling the memories of a person, place, or thing and the context of their time and times.

In 1817, the poet John Keats stated uncertainty to be a "creative gift of negative capability." He declared that uncertainty is a vital force in writing, and can empower one's capability of being with uncertainty as both dynamic and essential to present moment fact (fiction) and reason.